HOME
THIS
AFTERNOON

edited by JACK SINGLETON

drawings by David Knight

published by arrangement with
The British Broadcasting Corporation

LUTTERWORTH PRESS

LONDON

First published 1966

PRINTED IN GREAT BRITAIN
BY EBENEZER BAYLIS AND SON, LTD.
THE TRINITY PRESS, WORCESTER, AND LONDON

Contents

CONTENTS

FARAWAY PLACES

BIRDS AND BEASTS

A BREATH OF FRESH AIR

WAR YEARS

A CHRISTMAS HAMPER

USEFUL PUBLICATIONS

USEFUL ADDRESSES

ILLUSTRATIONS

Acknowledgements

The Publishers wish to thank the following for permission to reproduce photographs of which they hold the copyright: Aerofilms (7a, 8a); Brighton Museum (5b, 12, 14b); British Travel Association (6b); Council of Industrial Design (16); Michael Foxell (24); Gordon Fraser Gallery (2b); Guildhall Library (17); Therle Hughes (10, 11, 13, 14a): Henry E. Huntington Library and Art Gallery, California (18); London Museum (4b, 9, 19); Mansell Collection (2a, 3b); National Portrait Gallery (3a, 4a, 5a, 6a, 7b, 8b); Radio Times Hulton Picture Library (1, 20, 21, 22a and b, 23a and b); Wedgwood (15). The endpaper is based on a photograph of the village of Witley, near Godalming, Surrey, taken by Thomas A. Wilkie.

Foreword

THIS anthology is based on the B.B.C. Radio programme *Home This Afternoon*, which is heard by nearly half a million listeners every weekday. Now to pluck a voice from the air and put it into print is not easy, and sometimes it is impossible. News becomes history by the date of publication. The hot cut and thrust of an argument, say on trade unions or fluoridation, looks cold in black and white. A printed interview, like Ezekiel's dry bones, lacks the breath of life.

But in a magazine programme using almost every kind of radio presentation there are some items that come as lively off the page as on the air, and the best of these I have culled for this gift-book. The urbanity of Basil Boothroyd is revealed as much in the style of his writing as in the tone of his voice; the humour and pathos of Molly Weir's childhood memories can be enjoyed independent of her chirpy Glasgow accent; and the drama of a well-told tale such as *"Caucasian* and *U.39"* speaks for itself. Then too, when you are reading something by a friend—and many listeners look upon contributors to *Home This Afternoon* as friends—you read with your ears. The familiar voice is heard in the written word.

Variety is the spice of life, and it is also the secret of making an anthology. In this gift-book will be found professionals, whose names are household words, side by side with those who work at a corner of the kitchen table—writing about the good old days and the bad old days, the homely and the exotic, fish and chips and caviare, industrial slum and vice-regal lodge, Blackpool sands and Black Mountain fiord. But variety in itself is not enough, each item bears the distinctive hallmark that makes the anthology *Home This Afternoon.*

I would like to thank my B.B.C. colleagues, the contributors, and the editors of the Lutterworth Press for their co-operation in producing this book, through which, I hope, readers who are already listeners will enjoy again their favourite talks, and those who are not will be tempted from now on to tune in at a quarter to five on the Home Service every weekday.

JACK SINGLETON

ALL OUR YESTERDAYS

Frying Tonight

---

by Bill Taylor

AT THE TURN of the century my mother—a widow—kept the fried fish and chip shop in Percy Street, Neepsend, and Neepsend in those days was one of the poorest districts in Sheffield.

There were just three of us, my mother, our Sarah, and me. And our home was known simply as The Chip Shop.

Soon after I started school the lads christened me *Chips'n*. I realize now that I ought to have been flattered, for in those days boys liked nothing better than "chips 'n' fish". But I didn't like my nickname any more than James Stevenson who lived in Haddon Street liked his. He was called Four Eyes because he wore glasses. Still, I was blessed indeed compared with Peter Potter who was nicknamed Pee Pot.

My mother was a Yorkshire woman who honestly believed hard work killed nobody. Her own life hardly served to illustrate her claim. My father died shortly after I came on the scene, and she worked doubly hard to make a living and died in her middle fifties.

She was born too early to benefit from compulsory free education. Her parents, whom I never knew, were too poor to afford the odd coppers needed in those days for buying that "little larning" which was limited to reading, writing, and the most elementary arithmetic. She, poor dear, could neither read nor write. All the same, my mother's lack of schooling proved to be no drawback so far as running the shop was concerned. You see, my sister was a capable little body and kept the few records that were necessary by jotting down items on pieces of paper torn from flour bags and pinning them to the inside of a cupboard door.

Sarah was almost twenty years older than me, which has left me with the life-long suspicion that I was something of a mistake. The neighbours would most likely have described her as a "reight nice lass, wi' plenty of oil in her can"—meaning a lot of common-sense. To this, add a round, comely face, kindly grey eyes, and long black hair.

At thirteen she was employed by a firm which devoted much of its manufacture to making handsome cases for expensive sets of cut-throat razors, and although no one in those days talked of "metal fatigue" it was generally understood that a razor became "tired" if it was used too frequently, in other words the cutting edge was impaired. So to overcome the problem, sets of seven razors were provided—one for each day of the week.

Such a luxury, of course, was far beyond the means of working men. In any case, they rarely shaved more than once a week. That was on Sunday, the day they changed their flat caps, knotted scarves, and corduroys for their best clothes.

But to go back to our Sarah. . . . She had a two-fold duty at work. She helped in the making of the cases by heating glue; she also warmed dinners and mashed tea for the bench-hands.

As a baby, when the shop was open, I sat behind the counter in my high chair until Sarah came home. It was her job to put me to bed. After a long day she would have a "bit o' summat" to eat, then, putting on a clean pinny, go into the shop to serve, while mother attended to the frying.

The shop, which would normally have been the front room, had little interest for me until I started school. It was then that my mother said: "Cum, lad! It's time tha wa' earnin' thi keep."

I did this by cutting newspapers into squares to wrap the fish and chips, and filling the vinegar bottles from the cask under the counter. I also set out penny and twopenny bottles of Henderson's Yorkshire Relish. These bottles, I remember, had excessively long, thin necks and the corks were sealed with blobs of red sealing wax.

In addition to fish and chips we sold hot peas, bottles of mineral waters, ginger-beer in stone bottles, and bundles of firewood. On certain days there was tripe; it spilled over the top of a deep enamel bowl in rich, seamy flounces. There were pigs' trotters, rising in a pyramid from a large oval meat dish, and sometimes fish roe, looking like dunes of pale-gold sand, displayed on long tin trays.

The potatoes for the chips were peeled by hand—at least two hundred-weight for each day. They were kept in water in huge brown earthenware tubs highly glazed on the inside and known locally as "maiden pots". This, I believe, was a corruption of their original name of "made-in pots", the name given to utensils for mashing cattle food on farms.

The time came when I was expected to do *my* share of potato peeling. I'm bound to admit my efforts weren't successful. First I got into trouble for not taking out the eyes, then when I did take them out I got into trouble for cutting away too much of the potato.

"Nay, lad," Mother said, "if tha goes on at this rate we'll end up in t'work'us."

This wasn't meant as a joke for the Workhouse, Poor House, or Union as it was sometimes called, was a grim prospect indeed. It marked the bleak, inhospitable Journey's End of those without means. To many it meant an intolerable disgrace. To avoid this I was only called on to peel potatoes in emergencies.

Sarah used to say that my mother was as stubborn as a mule. She was certainly conservative; when frying in oil was first introduced she couldn't be persuaded to use it.

"Nay, it can't be wholesome," she said. "I've allus fried i' fat, an' them as wants oil mun go wheer they can get it."

The Chip Shop, however, was up-to-date in one important respect— it was lit by gas. At that time many houses and shops had not advanced beyond paraffin lamps.

The shop made great demands on Mother. She was up at first light, "seein' ter things", as she put it. Before breakfast she had lit the kitchen fire, raked out the flues in the shop, and thoroughly cleaned the big pans with a block of scouring powder called Monkey Brand.

While Sarah was getting ready for work Mother did the "packin' up". This might be a meat and potato pie in a basin, or bread and a jug of hash. She also prepared a mashing of tea and sugar in a screw of paper. But there were times when she would confess to having "nowt in".

"Ee, Sarah Lizzie, tha' best buy a bit o' summat," she'd say, and with the twopence halfpenny Mother gave her Sarah usually bought three-ha'porth of boiled ham, a ha'porth of pickles, and a ha'porth of stale pastries.

Then with our Sarah at work and myself at school, Mother walked all the way to the fish market in Castle Folds to order fish for the day. She also shopped, scrubbed, washed, cooked and prepared the batter in great yellow bowls. If our next-door neighbour knocked on the fireback with the poker it meant that help of some kind was needed. "T'owd lass is 'appen took badly," she'd say, and she would hurry out to see what was amiss.

Frying started about six in the evening, but the shop opened earlier to allow customers to leave plates and basins with their orders for the first frying. These were collected nice and hot for the "Mester's" tea.

Most of the customers arrived, clutching big shabby purses fat with pence and pawn tickets. Sixpence bought a meal for an entire family, especially if they had the luck to get tail-pieces at the rate of five for twopence. Customers would often ask for "strap"—credit, that is. This was dispensed with discretion, the amount being chalked on a slate hanging on the wall.

My mother knew the lives of most of her customers intimately for in those days the Chip Shop was a meeting house which had considerable social significance. Over a ha'porth o' chips they discussed their problems, divulged their sorrows and shared their joys.

Most firms paid out wages on Saturdays, so by Fridays business in the shop had slackened. Our Sarah took this night off to do her "coortin' ".

16

She was going steady with Frank, a young man who worked as a maintenance fitter in the forge at Howells' Wincobank Works.

Mother viewed Sarah's courtship with some misgiving due to the prospect of losing such a competent helper, but this was offset somewhat by Frank's volunteering to help peel potatoes two or three times a week.

"Aye, it's a rum way to do thi coortin', but any road, it'll keep thi out o' mischief," she said.

On Saturdays—the busiest day of the week—it was more than my life was worth to stray far from the shop in case I was needed. This usually happened when I was playing Touch-me-Last round the lamp-posts or hopscotching on the flags.

"Cum on, Chips'n!" someone would shout. "Mek haste! Thi muther wants thi ter chip some taters."

I'm ashamed to say I responded most reluctantly. I had to stand on an empty ginger-beer box to reach the heavy iron lever that worked the cutting blades, and (as my mother often said) I was "nowt but skin and bone". Chipping potatoes took all my strength, but there was *some* measure of satisfaction in watching the long, pale fingers falling into the colander below.

When the shop was full it was like Bedlam, especially when the raw chips were emptied into the deep fat. There was a terrific *hiss*, then a steady *s-i-z-z-l-e*, which almost drowned the lively chatter of the customers. Then the blue smoke belched across the shop and drifted through the open doorway into the street. Nostrils sniffed their appreciation, and small fingers tugged at heavy skirts. "Muther, can I 'ave sum chips?" Hands groped for coppers on mantelpieces; folk came out of the narrow entries . . . women in head-shawls . . . youngsters with protectors on their boots, sparking the cobblestones as they skittered along . . . men in corduroys saluted their neighbours with a ponderous " 'Ow do?" . . .

There were no winking neon signs; no luring, floodlit façade—simply the warm, pungent, friendly smell which would tell them the Chip Shop on Percy Street was Frying Tonight . . .

The 'Varsity

by Basil Boothroyd

I WONDER IF PEOPLE still talk about "The 'Varsity"? I hope not. It's hard to believe they ever did, somehow. There probably isn't another word in the language so packed with instant class and built-in privilege, and if it's vanished from circulation it's not before time.

But all that doesn't alter the fact that I'd have given my ears to have been a 'Varsity Man—which means Oxford or Cambridge only, of course; you wouldn't have caught me looking twice at Leeds or Leicester, nothing but the best for me—but of course I never had the chance. And when I say that, I hope you don't hear a whining note in the voice, because it's not supposed to be there. I'm not complaining in the least. It was simply a matter of fact that I didn't go. Well, two facts. I hadn't the brains, and the family hadn't the money.

At the time, when I was about twenty, I probably wouldn't have given it another thought . . . but it so happened that the bank I was in sent me to its Cambridge branch, and I somehow got in with a bunch of, well, you know, 'Varsity Men. I forget how it happened now—oh, yes, I know— the vicar's son from home was up at the university, and I suppose it seemed a properly Christian act for him to ask me to tea, or possibly beer, I forget which. If it was beer he bought it, because I think I was earning £6 a month at the time, and paying thirty bob a week for digs; so it didn't leave much beer money, especially in a five-week month. He introduced me to a rich Indian student—I used to say "a rich Indian prince" for a few years afterwards when I was talking about all this, but he's somehow got demoted since then. The thing about this prince—

18

Indian, I mean—was that he owned about sixteen musical instruments, drums, saxophones, trombones, trumpets, xylophones . . . enough stuff to equip the Savoy Orpheans, who were topping all the charts in those days. He was absolutely dotty on jazz, in fact, and so, as it happened, was I. The only difference between us was that he had all this glittering kit, and he couldn't play more than about two notes on any of it, and all I had was a nasty little nickel-plated soprano saxophone, the smallest and cheapest of the saxophone family, and—between you and me—I wasn't half bad on it. All we really needed to have a band was this chap's instruments, me, and about eight other people to play the rest of them. Where would anyone find this talented company, of course, but from some other 'Varsity Men? Which is just what happened.

So, for me, this very odd existence began. For about a year, I suppose, I was to all intents and purposes an undergraduate at Cambridge. Well, not to *all* intents and purposes. I didn't attend any lectures, for instance. But then I never heard that they did, either. And also it was often a bit difficult for me to attend afternoon engagements with the band, because there was this maddening business of having to be at the bank all day, which struck me as extremely unfair. Then again, of course, when it came to bump suppers and May Week balls and debates in the Union I was somewhat left out of it, naturally. Otherwise we were inseparable. We went up the river to Grantchester together, playing water music from punts, and if they all decided it would be amusing to climb a tree on the shore and jump into the water fully clothed, I was in there with the rest of them. Mind you, I probably hadn't any more clothes, and they had— but there you are, you can't have everything. They always made out they were very jealous of *me*. I was out in the world, earning a living, for one thing. Also I didn't have to take any examinations; and if for some reason the proctor's men came after us and took our names . . . well, I didn't have to give mine. I had full 'Varsity Man status with the girls, as well. "What college are you?" they sometimes asked, when our punts had just happened to collide—and I was quite honest, I used to give them the name of the bank. They were none the wiser, as far as I could ever see.

But it had to end, of course. The Cambridge manager thought I should do better at some other branch. I don't know why. Perhaps it was because he kept finding me asleep on the postage desk, and I don't think he liked me waving to the customers when members of the band came in. So I went off to the wilds of Lincolnshire after that, and started a band of my own. It was a bit different from the 'Varsity life but you're pretty adaptable at twenty. I soon got used to it.

And yet, you know, even now, I still feel conscious of a great gulf between the university man and—well, me. If I'm at some do or other, or perhaps just talking in the club, someone's only got to say, "When I was at Oxford"—or Cambridge—and a sense of inferiority starts creeping over me. It doesn't matter how they got there, or what they did there, or whether they were sent down or stayed up, or were somewhere splendid like King's or Magdalen, or somewhere crummy like—well, I'd better not say—they still carry this mystical accolade. And the odd thing is that nowadays I'm sometimes bidden to Oxford or Cambridge to speak to some College or University Society, or sometimes just to dine and not speak, which is even better . . . and what's odd about it is how very young and pink and beardless and unsophisticated and respectful these children are. There, in that setting of old grey stones and panelled rooms and silver candelabra and old masters—and positively primeval toilet facilities—they simply assume that I'm one of them. Well, just a minute, I've always assumed they assume . . . I mean, they never ask me. But I'm just wondering —and it's a chilling thought that's never occurred to me before—perhaps they can see at a glance that I'm not; perhaps they can tell from the very way my hair grows, or something, that I've never been a 'Varsity Man at all? Now I think of it, I shouldn't be a bit surprised. I'm quite prepared to believe that there's an outward and visible sign that marks out the elect, and that I haven't got it. One short year as an extramural under-graduate, reading jazz, beer and punting, simply isn't enough.

Oh, well, it's too late now. Other things I've missed I might still catch up with. But at my age, if you haven't been to a university, you've left it too late. It's a pity. But I've just got to lump it now.

The Fever Van

by Molly Weir

IN MY CHILDHOOD days in Glasgow the sight of the "fever van" struck a chill into our young hearts; but curiosity was always stronger than fear. We would gather on the pavement, ignoring the exhortations of our mothers, as we waited to catch a glimpse of a swathed figure on its way through the close to the ambulance, and shudder with relief that it wasn't us on the stretcher.

We lived in crowded tenements, and the mere whisper of fever, that infant scourge, sent mothers sick with dread, for, with twelve families to a close, infection could spread like wildfire. Awed as we children were by the sight of our playmates magically transformed to terrifying bundles borne on stretchers, we realized that while we were lively and healthy we might as well enjoy ourselves, and give a bit of help at the same time, and we organized backcourt concerts to raise money to buy presents for the hospital cases.

As soon as the ambulance had disappeared, we'd race through the close to the backcourt and decide on our entertainment. We'd perhaps arrange to do a rough imitation of the pantomime we'd seen from the gallery during the winter, or a cowboys and Indians episode from the latest film, and we had to decide whether our costumes would be made from crinkled paper or cast-offs begged from our mothers. We'd divide out the parts, and we sewed and pinned and rehearsed for days, practically in a fever ourselves, as we got everything ready for the big day. We never repeated a show—it had to be a full-scale new production for each victim.

We charged a halfpenny for children and a penny for adults, the adults sitting on the stone edging which ran round the backcourt railings, and the children sitting on the ground or standing, just as they pleased. We generally gave two performances, and our audience usually stayed for both, and were highly critical if they didn't get an exact repeat performance at the second house, word for word, gesture for gesture. As nothing was written down, and everything had been rehearsed on the principle of "You say this", and "I'll say that", this wasn't easy, but we pacified them by singing an extra verse of a favourite ditty if the mood turned ugly!

I gained valuable acting experience from these plays, and, although very nervous, was drunk with power when I discovered how easy it was to change the mood of the audience from one of enthusiastic delight at my swash-buckling impersonation of a principal boy, to silent pathos at my rendering of "Won't you buy my pretty flowers". It was heady stuff for a ten-year-old, and I must admit I quite forgot the victim in my enthusiastic production of my all-talking, all-singing, all-dancing extravaganzas.

We usually collected enough in pennies and halfpennies to be able to offer the fever victim a huge box of chocolates and a bag of fruit, and these shopping expeditions were in themselves a source of intense pleasure —we felt like millionaires as we crowded into the sweet-shop and selected, with great care, a box with a sympathetic dog on the lid, and then moved to the fruit shop next door where we spent the rest of the money on as many apples and oranges as the kitty would cover. No fanciful things like grapes or melons for us—oranges and apples were our limit and we knew they would be appreciated to the last bite.

Somehow in all this activity, one always assumed it would be someone else who would be chosen for the victim, and the part of the entertainer would be filled by oneself. Then, the one year when we simply couldn't afford it to happen, the fever-germ struck our house, and it struck me. My aunt was home on a visit from Australia on a specially reduced ticket which involved her travelling back by a certain date. If she went beyond this date an extra £20 had to be paid, an enormous sum in our world. She had come home to have her last baby born in Scotland, and we were within three weeks of her sailing, when I came home complaining of a sore throat and a throbbing head. I didn't know what these symptoms meant, but my mother and my grannie did. I caught the look of horror which passed between them, and I was puzzled. They didn't speak, beyond handing me a glass, pouring in some stuff and telling me to gargle. As I was tucked into bed, I heard Auntie whisper, "We ought to send for the doctor." My mother shushed her fiercely. "We can't. You'd never be allowed to leave, and you must get that boat. Where could we get twenty pounds?" "But Jeanie," my auntie urged, "she should be in hospital." Hospital! Ambulances! I was to be the next bundle carried through the gaping spectators! I felt the tears sting my eyelids at the thought of it, but my mother would have none of it. "I can do what's necessary," she said.

Now at that time in our small room-and-kitchen tenement flat there were three adults, three children and an infant, and the toilet was outside on the stair and had to be shared with two other families, so the risk of infection spreading was terrifying. But my mother faced it all, and took it in her stride. She was used to hardship, and used to battling with difficulties, with poverty as the spur, and in this crisis she was magnificent. She had her job in a motor-works to attend to, for she was a widow, responsible for the three children, but she saw that everything I touched or used was sterilized. She was so powerful and dramatic when she explained to my brothers about the dangers of using anything I had eaten from, that for months afterwards they refused to drink from a cup if they had seen it anywhere near my bed during my illness. Gargling routines were punctiliously observed, light diet adhered to, and as I slept with Grannie we felt it was most unlikely she would be infected at her age.

The worst part was trying to keep my school chums from visiting me. We couldn't and daren't tell them the real cause of my illness, but we couldn't risk suspicion and the dreaded "sanitary" descending upon us by refusing everyone admittance. So the one or two bosom chums who couldn't be kept out were made to sit at the other end of the kitchen and yell their sympathy from there, on the excuse that I was very easily made to sneeze, and the cold air that came in with them brought on an attack. Strange to say, everyone believed this, for they were a trusting community. Even I wasn't sure that it was the fever I had (for the word was never mentioned), until the skin began to peel in strips from my hands, and then I wore little white silk gloves and pretended that I did so because I liked to keep my hands outside the bed-clothes and when they got cold again it made me sneeze. Once more, because I had always been full of mad capers and loved dressing up, everyone believed us.

The new baby was kept in the other room, and I never saw her again, except held at a distance at the other end of the kitchen, just before she left with Auntie for the boat. Auntie gazed at me compassionately and lovingly, but didn't come nearer to say goodbye.

It was a miracle, of course, but our efforts were crowned with complete success. Nobody else on our stair developed even the mildest symptom. I gradually found my strength, and at last was ready for school again. My absence had been explained as prolonged bronchitis, and as I was always top of the class and a fervently enthusiastic pupil, nobody doubted us. But there was a terrible moment when I went back to school and the teacher looked up from the register as I answered "Present, Miss". "Oh hullo dear. Are you better? Was it the fever?"

I stared at her dumbly, the blood rushing to my pale cheeks. "How had she guessed? What would I say?" It was one thing acting a lie, especially when I hadn't really known it was a lie for a long time, but quite another putting it into words. Then she consulted the register again, with its marginal notes. "Oh no, bronchitis I see. Are you sure you're better? You look very congested to me." Congested! I was on the point of fainting with fear, followed by relief.

So even into the school register our deception had succeeded, succeeded so well in fact, that I didn't have a single "benefit" concert. There were no chocolates or fruit for bronchitis, only for scarlet fever and I hadn't had scarlet fever. Or had I?

But if I hadn't had the chocolates, I hadn't had the ride in the dreaded "fever van" either, and that experience I gladly foreswore.

24

STREET
CRIES
THROUGH
THE
CENTURIES

Ever since towns existed we can reasonably assume that some traders sold goods by crying their wares in the street. The author of the 14th-century poem 'London Lackpenny' describes the noisy scene of peddlers crying 'Hot pescod', 'Strabery rype and cherry in the tyse', 'Great chepe clothe' and 'Hot shepes fete'. In Queen Elizabeth's day Gibbons, Weelkes and Deering set some of the cries to music—'Quick periwinkles quick quick quick', 'Fine Sevil oranges fine leamons', 'Sweet juniper juniper will you buy my bunch of juniper', 'I ha' ripe cowcumbers ripe'. Victorian London was crowded with street salesmen as Mayhew and others have described.

Today mass production and supermarkets have almost eliminated the street crier, yet he is not quite extinct. The gipsy woman selling lavender and primroses, the rag-and-bone man, the fruit stallholder, the winkle-barrow-boy and the hot chestnut roaster still shout incomprehensibly, and the chimes of the ice-cream van bring children running out of their homes to buy.

Four engravings from a book entitled *The Manner of Crying Things in London*, published about 1599.

A hot pudding seller drawn by Paul Sandby in 1759. This is one of an attractive series of 'London Cries' depicted by an artist who is well known as a water-colourist. They are exhibited at the London Museum.

A milk-maid of 1805.

THE STREET-SELLER OF GREASE-REMOVING COMPOSITION, ETC.

THE LUCIFER MATCH GIRL.

THE GROUNDSEL MAN.

THE COSTER-GIRL.

A selection of four illustrations from 'London Street Folk', volume 2 of *London Labour and the London Poor* by Henry Mayhew, published in 1861.

Four London scenes showing a knife-grinder, a shoe-black in Fleet Street, a man selling a cool drink of fruit juice in Cheapside, and a girl who might be taken as a model for Eliza in Shaw's *Pygmalion*. The photographs were taken by Paul Martin in 1900.

Most street selling is now confined to markets where salesmen raucously invite buyers and entertain the casual passer-by. However, the hot-chestnut barrow still does a good trade on a cold winter's day as it has done for centuries, and the cry of winkles and cockles through the streets of the East End of London brings eager customers to buy their traditional Sunday tea.

The Train With The Tartan Engine

by Leslie Gardiner

SHE LIES, OR she was lying a few years ago, in pieces among a heap of scrap metal in a rural goods yard of Aberdeenshire: Tank Locomotive Number Two of the old Deeside railway. Country folk called her Meldrum Meg, after she came off the main routes to end her days shunting up and down the branch line between Old Meldrum and Inverurie. But to an earlier generation she was the *Queen's Messenger*, the one and only tartan locomotive.

The tale of the tartan locomotive begins just over a hundred years ago when the management of the newly-opened railway along the river Dee from Aberdeen wrote to Queen Victoria and offered to deliver her mail to Balmoral. At that time, whenever the Royal Family was in Scotland, despatches were sent up every night by rail to Blairgowrie and then collected by a courier, who travelled over the hills in a pony and trap; the last fifty miles of his journey across the Devil's Elbow and through Glen Shee taking about twice as long as the first five hundred had done.

The railway company's idea was to collect the mail off the night train to Aberdeen and run it to Balmoral by special train. They evidently regarded it as a prestige job: they proposed to charge only nine pounds for the train's double journey of eighty miles, and that would include breakfast for the courier and the cost of a carriage and pair between the nearest station and the castle.

The *Queen's Messenger*, as the train was called, began as an experiment during the Queen's Scottish holiday of 1865 and never looked back. At first the small tank engine and its single Pullman coach could only go as far as Aboyne, thirty miles from Aberdeen. As soon as the full length of the Deeside railway was opened, it went on to Ballater, another ten, and that left the courier a mere seven or eight miles to travel with his horses to Balmoral. A note from Lord Derby or young Mr. Disraeli in London could be put in the big red despatch-box when Parliament rose in the evening and be on Her Majesty's early-morning tea-tray next day: an incredible rate of travel for that age and, indeed, one that has been scarcely bettered since.

Railway proprietors, especially on the scenic routes, vied with each other to produce not only the fastest time-tables but also the smartest brass and paint-work and the most eye-catching colour schemes. The Deeside trains, always among the most handsome, were tastefully picked out in royal blue and black. Their engines had burnished stovepipe chimneys and gleaming brass domes and were renowned for their immaculate polish. It must have come as a shock to folk along the line when the *Queen's Messenger* started running with a bright purple and gold coach and the imperial cypher on its panels; even more of a shock when Tank Locomotive Number Two pulled it—an engine painted in tartan stripes, and no restrained variety of tartan either but the Royal Stuart, brilliant with reds and whites and blues.

"Tartanitis" had just hit Balmoral, all the court and half the nation was down with it, and this was supposed to be a compliment to Her Majesty. But milk-maids on Deeside complained their cattle were not giving the yield they used to, since the tartan train started running: it came down to Ballater about milking time.

The *Queen's Messenger* was never a great tourist attraction. Not many people cared to turn out at four o'clock in the morning, even to see a tartan engine go by. But it had its place in legal history: at the beginning of its long run it figured in a much-publicized and extremely costly lawsuit. In the charter granted to the railway company, all their passenger trains were required to stop at Crathes, an insignificant wayside platform. The company refused to halt the *Queen's Messenger* there, arguing that there would be no passengers for it at that hour of the day and that it was not a passenger train within the meaning of the term anyway. The case dragged on for years, went to the House of Lords in the end, and the railway company lost.

Originally the tartan train carried the Queen's courier alone, locked up with his despatches and a luxurious coach all to himself. Then a second coach was added, for guests and staff coming off the London express and bound for Balmoral. Finally members of the public were allowed to use the train and a third-class coach was added, for servants and luggage. The Deeside line changed hands over the years, new stations were built and old ones dismantled, monarchs came and went, the signatories to the precious despatches altered with the times . . . and still the "Messenger" ran on, *King's Messenger* now, whenever the court was in residence at Balmoral, right up to the year 1937.

Then they went back to the old system: night train to Blairgowrie and over the hills, in a car this time. Nowadays the Queen's despatch-box is delivered to Balmoral by helicopter—sometimes more quickly, sometimes more slowly, never more picturesquely, than in the bright tartan days of the Deeside "Messenger".

Scholarship Boy

by Joe Hoyland

SOME FIFTY YEARS ago, I went to a Council school in the North and so far as the schooling itself went, I was very happy indeed. The school was in a district inhabited chiefly by craftsmen; engineers, carpenters, electricians and so on, and these people were fairly prosperous at that time. Their children attended the same school as myself, and were generally well-fed, decently clothed and shod. But I simply didn't belong in this atmosphere and through no fault of my own.

I was an only child. My father died when I was quite young; my mother was semi-invalid and couldn't work. We shared a two-up and two-down house with another family; my mother paid 2/- per week rent; Parish relief just about kept us alive, and for clothing Mother kept me going with whatever cast-offs she could lay hands on.

One day I said, "Why can't I go to Dyson Street school, Ma, instead of walking all the way to Fretton." Ma looked at me quite sympathetically, "I want you to stay at Fretton, it's the best school in this town and when you leave Fretton, you'll be fit for a job anywhere—you know what I mean, a nice collar-and-tie job. There'll be no need to go into any of the factories and you'll be able to hold your head high."

I liked Fretton as a school, but although quite young, I was more than conscious of the fact that there wasn't one child in my class who was so ill-clad as I. This alone was why I asked Ma if I could change schools and it was a matter of such concern to me that I decided to pursue the idea further.

"It's three miles to Fretton, Ma, three miles there and three miles back;

that's six miles every day and look at the boot leather I'd save if I went to Dyson, that's only around the corner."

"That's quite right, Joe," she said, "but somehow or other, we'll manage it. You work hard at Fretton and in years to come, you'll be glad you did as I said."

I asked on more than one occasion later, but she persuaded me gently but firmly, to stay at the one school, and as Ma and I were close together, I couldn't bring myself to tell her the real reason for wanting a change, because I knew this would hurt her deeply.

I went to school and home again alone, wandered around the playground at playtime and stayed in at lunch time, eating my bread and syrup sandwiches in the cloakroom. I did have a slight edge on my school fellows, however, because I was fairly bright and when exams came around for class placings, I worked like fury because nothing short of top of the class would suit me, and I pulled it off regularly.

This also helped me materially, because sitting next to me in school was a not-so-bright boy whose parents kept a sweet shop. He loathed arithmetic and I was considerably flattered when he said to me one playtime, "I say, Hoyland," (not Joe, by the way—he was still keeping me at a social distance), "you're good at sums and you're always finished before me, so if you'll copy the work on a piece of paper and slip it to me when teacher isn't looking, it'll save me a roasting. I'll bring you a bag of sweets in the morning." I was really thrilled by the admission that at last I was someone who was useful, whilst sweets thrown in as part of the bargain was beyond my dreams.

I agreed and when the terminal exams came around, he stepped his bribery up by offering me a penny in addition to the sweets, but I stopped at exam answers; I wanted to be top and wasn't taking any chances with him or anybody else. I let him know just where I stood and I was surprised he didn't press because I was fearing inwardly that he might try to frighten me by threatening to tell about my helping him previously.

My stock soared appreciably when I was picked for the school football team and when we won the schools' championship, the team were called up to the platform in the hall where the shield was proudly displayed. It was a moment of glory indeed. Being "Joe Rags", as I knew I was called behind my back, didn't bother me in the least for here I was, as good as anybody and one of eleven who were, at the moment at least, better than everybody else. The Head lauded us to the skies and when the whole school gave three cheers for the football team, the thrill was past descriptive powers.

There were no eleven-plus exams in those days and the only access to education beyond the age of fourteen was, in our school at least, to pass a qualifying exam for what was called the "Higher Grade" and this was for boys only. The elevation to higher classes was only on the basis of ability and not age, hence, there were some children who left school at the age of fourteen in Standard 2, who on their age rating, should have been in Standard 7.

By the age of fourteen, I was in Standard 7 plus, which meant that I could sit for the Higher Grade exam to stay on at school until I was sixteen. The object of this was for boys to go straight from school to an apprenticeship or for training in commerce. I was delighted when my name was called out and felt sure that I could qualify.

A few days before the exam, one of my boots, which were in very poor condition, fell to pieces and this was a shattering blow for me. Whilst some schools in the town allowed attendance in bare feet, my school at Fretton would not tolerate this and in spite of Ma reassuring me that something would turn up, I was utterly despondent. The night before the exam, nothing had turned up, so I told Ma that I would go to school barefoot and chance the consequences. "You can't do that, Joe," she said, "you'll only be sent home and that would hurt both you and me more than anything else." I cried myself to sleep that night, I desperately wanted to sit that exam, but there seemed no hope.

I got up as usual next morning and Ma said, "There'll be no school for you today, Joe; you can't go barefooted. I'll get you something by the weekend and you'll be all right for next week." Then an idea struck me, and I said triumphantly, "I'm going, Ma and I'm going to pass." Ma looked at me in a stupefied way, "But how are you going to——" I cut her short. "I'm going in your boots and don't try to stop me; now don't," I repeated.

I put Ma's high-legged, lace-up boots on, gave them a mirror shine and went off to school, whistling gaily. The happy feeling evaporated as soon as I went into the playground when one bright spark passed a remark about a fire-bobby coming to school. This was number one of four fights I had before going into school with my hair bedraggled, a dirty face, swollen lip, bloody nose, and clothes covered in dust; a very sorry spectacle indeed. But I passed the exam—and with flying colours at that.

I went home and told Ma I'd passed and could go on into the Higher Grade and that the Head had said that I would need seven and sixpence for my first set of books. I can see Ma's face now as she said to me, "We haven't seven and sixpence for bread, let alone books"; then she threw her arms around me and cried.

So ended my hopes of further education and on the very day that I was fourteen, I left school and got a job pulling a handcart around.

On reflection, I am very happy with the thought that today ability and will are the only things necessary to achieve any educational ambition.

Having Your Throat Cut

by Alan Paget

TODAY THE MEDICAL profession claims to have
registered an encouraging measure of success in its perennial offensive
against that most persistent of British afflictions, the common cold; but
in the early years of the century the picture was not so rosy. Regularly
every winter my little sister and I fell victims to what is now euphemisti-
cally called catarrh. It involved a stuffy nose, a raw and painful throat
and a distressing tendency to violent snoring at night, which deprived our
devoted nannie of many hours of well-earned sleep. Our parents were
naturally much concerned and every morning our "Mummy", as we
called her, came up to our nursery on the top floor of the tall house in
South Kensington to administer treatment. This consisted first in having
to sniff up a solution of witch-hazel, which caused a violent pain at the
back of the head. Then we had our tonsils thoroughly swilled with a
brush soaked in a stinging brown liquid which nearly made us sick.
Altogether we came to dread these early morning visitations, much as
we loved our Mummy.

The time came when our devoted and untiring mother must have seen
that her ministrations were not having the desired effect. I can only suppose
that she and Daddy discussed the matter and eventually considered the
idea of a tonsils-and-adenoids operation. Naturally no word of this was
breathed to us children, but, as children will, we managed to overhear a
word or two—and the operative word was "cut". Thereafter, whenever
we were beset by colds and sore throats, we used anxiously to assail
Mummy for assurances that we were not going to "have our throats cut",

as we came to call it. We may well have had some justification for this instinctive fear. Operations in those days were quite often performed at home and were not the well-ordered, astringent, clinically slick affairs they are today.

The day came when nannie, with a rather peculiar expression on her face, told us we were not going to get up that morning, nor were we to have any breakfast. Very soon my mother appeared accompanied by my father, making one of his rare appearances in the nursery. I no longer remember what they said, but they left us with the impression we were good little dears and everything was going to be all right. Nannie then put on my dressing gown and took me away to another room, and I think she began to tell me a story. After a while I was taken back to the nursery where I found that the table had been moved into the middle of the room and there were a pillow and blankets on it. I was lifted on to the table and laid on my back. Then the nursery door opened and three big men in frock coats marched in and deposited their top hats on a chair. They went over to the fireplace, two of them carrying little black bags, out of which we had been led to believe they were in the habit of producing babies. On this occasion they must merely have contained instruments, and I suppose they were sterilizing them in the only way possible which was by putting them into the nursery kettle which was already boiling on the coal fire. They whispered together for a few moments, then one of them put on a pair of steel-rimmed spectacles and looked towards the windows and then at me on the table. It was a bright morning and apparently they thought the light was all right for whatever they had in mind, which was fortunate because the only other means of illumination was a bare bats-wing gas jet above the mantelpiece. Downstairs, of course, they had the new incandescent gas-mantle which burned inside a glass chimney and gave a brilliant white light which everyone admired.

One of the men then came to the table and clapped something like a half coconut shell over my mouth and nose. It was a horrid, suffocating feeling and I couldn't imagine what he was up to. Naturally I tried to pull it away, but someone held my hands down. I found out afterwards that it was Daddy who had come up to watch the proceedings. Gazing up at the ceiling, I remember wondering whether I should scream or lie quiet. I can recall the pattern on the ceiling to this day.

The next thing I knew was that I was still on the table and a hand towel all covered with blood was lying at my side. The man, who was now in his shirt-sleeves with his cuffs rolled back, quickly snatched the towel away. Of course none of the men wore the white gown, skull cap, mask and rubber gloves without which no surgeon would think of operating today. They poured some of the hot water from the kettle into the basin on the wash-stand in which they rinsed their hands and instruments and dried them on a towel. Then they put on their black coats again, picked up their top hats and went away.

I was now back in my cot, and my sister, who had had first turn on the table, was next to me in hers. The whole room was permeated with the sickly sweet odour of ether which hung about the nursery for days. Remembering the peculiar pungent smell of fresh print from the newspapers when we came downstairs to see our parents each morning, I begged to have one given to me now. Nannie, dear soul, brought one up and I kept sniffing it with relish. I now wonder if this early attraction for newsprint was a foreknowledge of later years when I grew up and became an engineer, and for a time edited a technical journal.

Strange though it may seem, we didn't realize we had had an operation. Dimly I imagined that the doctors had given us a sort of super throat painting, but neither of us knew we had "had our throats cut". We made a good recovery and it must have been some weeks later that my sister, who had been out for a walk one afternoon with mother, came rushing in to me with the news: "Mummy's just told me we did have our throats cut when the doctors were here!" My first reaction was naturally one of surprise, followed by a feeling that I'd been hoodwinked. Then we began to feel rather important at having had our throats cut. Anyhow, the thing was over and done with and no longer an ordeal to be feared.

There is an unexpected postscript to this story. The time is nineteen years later; March 1919 to be exact. I was back from the war and had applied for priority demobilization so that I could return to college. I was instructed to proceed to a certain house in South Kensington which the army had taken over. When I heard the number of the house in Queen's Gate I pricked up my ears and assured the presiding officer that I should have no difficulty in finding my way there. The exterior had changed hardly at all. The front door was ajar and I walked in. A clerk at a table in the tiled hall directed me to the top floor. I mounted the four flights, looked for the appropriate label on the door, and, sure enough, that was the room. So it came about that, now a young gunner officer home again at long last, I was demobilized in my own nursery, from the windows of which we had hung out little flags at the relief of Mafeking, and in the very room in which I had "had my throat cut". I wish I had remembered to look at the pattern of the paper on the ceiling.

Child's Eye View

by C. E. Salton

THE CHILD SWUNG her legs dejectedly in the hard pew. Framed in brown ringlets, her cheeks glowed cherry bright above the reefer coat, but her feet in black stockings and anklebands were frog cold and sorely chilblained. If only she could climb to the roof and dangle her legs from a rafter, she might forget about them; she could play a game of spotting people by the tops of their heads. Mr. Featherstone would be too easy; he had five pink lumps pushing up from bare, shiny patches in his hair.

No use to go on thinking about that. Better to watch the sunshine coming through the stained glass window and making lovely patterns on the flagstones; when she twirled a piece of orange peel underneath her heel in a pool she could make nearly the same pattern herself.

Looking at the hymn-board she turned up the numbers in her book and found one of her favourites: the one with the little bear in, "Can a woman's tender care, Cease towards the child she bear?" (she thought of it happily as dark-brown and furry). The Reverend's boots with such thick, thick soles coming from under his white surplice looked very queer: not at all like little mice peeping in and out as the poetry said. When he came to breakfast at Uncle's after Early Service, he nearly always asked for two very soft-boiled eggs. That was a pity because quite often he let the yellow drop down his beard; he should either have hard-boiled or shave off his beard. Aunt Nellie said he took drugs and slept with his housekeeper, but Mother said Aunt Nellie had a lewd mind. She liked to hear him read; he made the stories real and never said "he that hath yahs to yah, let him yah".

"He hath filled the hungry with good things and the rich he hath sent empty away." That was only fair. If the first could happen to Elsie Parker's seven children, they need not always eat bread and dripping; they could have eggs, butter and ham, and wine-trifle on Sundays; she liked to play with them, but not to sit by them at school, they so often smelled of sick. Mother said it was because their vests and things were not changed often enough. Mother was poor since Father died, but she was good. She would mend and wash grown-out clothes late at night and let her take them to the house next day. It was lovely to see Elsie's face when she opened the parcel.

As the Reverend clomped to the lectern she pricked her ears for the opening sentence of the lesson. Ah! Elijah on Mount Horeb—the Wind, the Fire, the Earthquake, the Still Small Voice; but best of all the little cakes, baked on the fire of coal by the kind angel. They made Elijah forget about being no better than his fathers, and wanting the Lord to take away his life, and made him strong to go after Ahab again. Elijah was a good prophet, not like Elisha who called for bears to eat up those children because they shouted, "Go up thou bald head." What a tale!

The cakes sent her mind forward to the coming dinner at Uncle's—roast duck, apple sauce and bottled peas (the garden ones were all gone), then Aunt Eliza's special trifle for children: brown bread soaked in wine and topped with raspberries and whipped cream. After dinner she would call for her friend Anson Ogley to walk to Thorpe Grange and see if the snowdrops were out in the orchard—thousands of them, single and double.

"Through the tender mercy of our God whereby the Dayspring from on High hath visited us." That sang like the piano when Aunt Nellie played "The Moonlight" and "Art Thou Troubled". Mr. Cargill (who had taught her) said she had everything but perseverance. "To give light to them that sit in darkness and in the shadow of death." People in prison sat in darkness she supposed, and those who lived by graveyards were in the shadow of death, but they did not seem to mind about it.

When Aunt Nellie let down her hair it looked like the golden rain willow tree in the sunshine; Mother had a photo with it like that. One day Aunt said to Mother that Doctor George's horse and the traveller's gig could stand an hour at Mother's gate and no one said a word—but there—her plain face saved her every time. So when Mother came home, she took the photo out of her album and said "Oh false-faced lying Jezebel that she is!" and tore it in pieces and put every piece on the fire. That seemed a shame for Aunt's face in the photo looked like the picture of Mary Queen of Scots in Aunt's front kitchen. But Mother was not plain, though her hair was only brown. Doctor George said it was a shame she could not wear evening dress and go into society, she had such pretty arms and shoulders.

"Time like an ever rolling stream bears all its sons away."

"A thousand ages in thy sight are like an evening gone." This eternity again! Never, never, never a million times never ending, and then not.

37

Baffled, she sought refuge in everyday matters. Would the two boys have cleaned out the rabbits whilst she was away? If not she wouldn't go on reading *Midshipman Easy* to them until they did. It was not so easy as reading to herself; Mother said she must miss out all the bad words that were not fit for the boys to hear, and that made her have to look on before to see what was coming. After all, she must not be too hard on them, like the Lord on Sodom and Gomorrah, only if she had to clean the hutches herself. Now Uncle was getting ready to take round the red velvet collecting bag (embroidered with gold thread) which she so longed for. Dutifully she slipped in the silver sixpence with which he had equipped her, and looked up for his nod of approval.

Now for the time being, her chilblains had ceased troubling and she stepped along the aisle happily enough to the march from *Alceste*. When her uncle had counted the collection in the vestry he joined her at the church gate. As she walked sedately by his side, her mind skipped forward to the evening when she would ask him to open the bookcase and take out the Cassel's *History* which told how the blood gushed from Catherine of Braganza's nose when Charles II presented Lady Castlemaine to her; there was a picture but it did not show the blood. Perhaps Uncle would have finished with *The Strand* by then and she could read *Story for Children*, and *Gleams from the Dark Continent*—even better it was than *Shafts from an Eastern Quiver*; if not she would go on with *East Lynne*. Aunt Eliza would say, "That is not a fit book for the child to read." But Uncle would say, "Oh! leave the bairn alone whatailsher." Lovely to be at Uncle's.

The Paper-chase

by John Anthony Parr

I WAS ABOUT seventeen years old at the time and the assistant scoutmaster of the village Boy Scout troop. I can't remember the exact year but most of the boys would by now be middle-aged and the fathers of families.

That summer we had a long spell of fine hot weather and so when the Scouts came and asked me whether I would arrange a paper-chase for the following Saturday I was only too happy to agree.

Saturday came and the entire troop turned up at our meeting place, the village school. It was arranged that I and three of the bigger boys should set out as the hares and lay the trail, and the rest of the Scouts should give us half an hour's start and then come hounding after us. After the paper-chase all the Scouts had to report back at the school for checking, and the inducement to report back was a free feed of buns and American Ice Cream Soda, which was their favourite drink.

I and my three helpers set off from the school at a loping trot down the hill and across the level crossing and through the fields towards the sand-pits. Giving the sandpits a wide berth, lest some of our following Scouts should fall in, we turned left by Mr. Mellors' farm and made for the open fields beyond, keeping close to the hedgerows to avoid damaging the crops.

It was a simply lovely day, the sun shone out of a clear blue sky; the hedges were smothered in wild roses whose soft gentle perfume filled the air; the dragonflies in shimmering colour darted along with us, and we were young and healthy and thoroughly enjoying ourselves.

We plodded on, scattering pieces of paper at intervals as we ran. Suddenly we came to a gap in the hedge and I decided to go through and lay the trail right across a sweeping meadow. The others followed and we ran lightly down an embankment. At the bottom was a series of curiously shaped rectangular concrete foundations, at least that is what they appeared to be, entirely covered with moss from being exposed to the air. Each of these concrete rectangles was about five feet across and twenty to thirty feet long. I decided to jump across the first one; after all five feet was no distance for the champion long-jumper of my boarding school. As I took off I was aware of a wailing voice from behind calling out, "Don't jump that, sir, please don't jump." The cry startled me and I looked down but it was too late; I was airborne. All the cry succeeded in doing was to make me hesitate and instead of clearing the five feet easily I only jumped four feet and landed not on the concrete foundation but in what proved to be an evaporating tank for the local sewage works.

It was only two feet deep so it only took an instant to scramble out—but the smell! It was intense, it was monumental, it was disgusting, it was diabolical. I stood there dumbfounded with my three Scouts standing at a respectful distance. One Scout capped the lot by wrinkling his nose and telling me . . . "Oh, sir, you do pong!" And believe me pong I did and no mistake.

There was only one thing for it—I'd have to go home. I sent one Scout back to the gap in the hedge to ward off the following Scout troop and gave the other two instructions to re-lay the trail well away from the sewage farm, whilst I ruefully set out the three miles for home.

My predicament was made worse by the realization of the awful reception I would get from my mother when I did get home. Not that she was unkind, far from it, but she was of Irish stock and both superstitious and fearful of germs. Germs to her always meant the "fever", and bad smells to her always meant germs; thus any noxious smell immediately conjured up to my mother the dire risk of catching the fever and that sent her slightly hysterical. And did I smell!

The extent of Mother's obsession about smells and the fever can be best illustrated by relating two incidents. The first happened the previous summer, when I had been home for the long summer holiday and spent a lot of time catching and bottling grass snakes in spirit. After I'd returned to school I received a letter from my mother. It simply said she doubted whether I'd be able to come home for the Christmas holiday as there was such a terrible smell and she was going to make Father have all the drains re-laid. The smell, she said, seemed to come from my bedroom and spread all over the house and already she'd had the plumber in to tear the bath waste pipes to pieces. It suddenly dawned on me that perhaps it was my snakes, so I went to my housemaster and poured out my fears and he sent Mother a laconic telegram which read:

"Do not smash the home up until you have looked in John's wardrobe."

It turned out that the spirit had evaporated from my grass snakes and so our main drainage was saved.

The next incident happened quite regularly at home. Whenever we left home to go by car to London we had to pass the local Fever Hospital, and for half a mile before we got to it and for half a mile after we had passed it, I and my sisters were made to bury our faces into our handkerchiefs and look away from the high wall round the hospital . . . "Lest you all catch the germs". To us, as children, germs were frightful things as big as stag-beetles which could do a half-roll over the hospital wall and attack us without mercy. Perhaps that's why I eventually became a doctor, just to deal the death blow at these monstrous stag-beetle things called germs which frightened mothers and children.

But to return to my baptism by sewage—with such a mother waiting for me you can imagine that, as I neared home, I dragged my steps a little.

Nevertheless I did arrive and, cautiously approaching the kitchen from the yard, called to Mother through the open door.

Mother gave one look at me and, smelling me at the same time, waited not an instant for an explanation but quickly slammed the door, and with her handkerchief close up to her nose, called out instructions through the closed window of the kitchen.

With some difficulty I managed to understand I was to go and get Sam, our gardener. He was to hose me down, then I was to drop all my clothes in the yard and go straight up to the bathroom.

I fetched the imperturbable Sam whose only comment was, "I could do with some of that there for mi' tomarters". Anyway with great gentleness he turned the hose on me and washed me down and then terribly embarrassed I dropped off my clothes and in my birthday suit opened the kitchen door.

I could hear Mother banishing our maid Bessie to her bedroom and through the dining room flap, which opened into the kitchen, Mother gave me my instructions—to keep to the newspaper she had laid on the floor and get straight into the bath.

Sheepishly I trotted across the kitchen, keeping to the newspapers which would stick to my wet feet. I got to the bathroom, to find the bath three parts full of hot water and reeking of disinfectant.

I was no sooner in the bath, than more instructions came through the closed door. I was "to get the worst off", empty the bath, and then refill it for a second soaking. The second bath was to be a mixture of hot water and scented bath salts which I'd find in the bathroom cupboard, after which I would find my clean clothes outside the bathroom door on the mat, and I was not to splash about and make a mess like Father did, as Bessie had cleaned the bathroom once that day, etc. etc. . . . I just closed my ears to the rest of the instructions and wallowed in the hot water.

Later I emerged clean and wholesome and not only clean but almost surgically sterile as well. Mother was very kind and sympathetic about my ordeal but by no means satisfied . . . germs were funny things she said, and you could never be entirely certain when dealing with them . . . and so nothing would satisfy her but that I got out my motorbike and went to see the family doctor five miles away, as she said, "He can give you some medicine which will clear your system."

Wearily I mounted my little two-stroke and set off to see Dr. Faulkner to "get some medicine to clear my system".

Fate hadn't finished with me yet; perhaps because I was overtired;

perhaps, because my mind was not on the road anyway, I skidded in some loose stones at one corner and came off. I remounted and with blood dripping from a cut eyebrow arrived at the village doctor's. He stitched me up and howled with glee at my sewage story and just had to fetch his partner so that I could tell the story all over again.

To this day I carry that scar on my left eyebrow and when I'm shaving sometimes I notice it and it conjures up the picture of that Boy Scout saying to me on that beautiful summer's day, almost forty years ago . . . "Oh, sir, you do pong".

Inscription on an old clock in Chester Cathedral

When as a child I laughed and wept,
   Time crept,
When as a youth I dreamed and talked,
   Time walked,
When I became a full grown man,
   Time ran,
And later, as I older grew,
   Time flew.
Soon I shall find while travelling on,
   Time gone.
Will Christ have saved my soul by then?
   Amen.

FAMILY ALBUM

The Peppermint Bible

by Lavinia Derwent

GRANNY'S FAMILY BIBLE always lay in the same spot on the window-sill, with her spectacles on top of it and a bag of peppermints at its side. Religion and peppermints seemed to go together in Granny's estimation. She liked to suck the one while pondering over the other; and now that she could no longer go to church, it gave her a feeling of taking part in the service if she popped a peppermint in her mouth on Sunday morning and opened the Bible at Proverbs.

I used to wonder why she made such a rite of putting on her spectacles since she never looked through them but always peered over the top. But they had belonged to her mother who wore them when reading the same Bible, and Granny liked to follow in her footsteps. "Besides, it would be a pity to waste them," she would say, thriftily.

There were pictures in Granny's Bible. I liked the Good Samaritan best of all, but Granny had a leaning towards Daniel because he reminded her of Uncle Andrew who had gone to America, which was little better than the Lions' Den, in her opinion!

Apart from its Biblical lore, Granny's Good Book contained treasures between almost every page, ranging from clippings of Uncle Andrew's baby-hair to recipes for curing the colic, from pictures of a long-ago Sunday School Treat to a pattern for a baby's vest.

Granny would begin by reading to me the story of Joseph and his Brethren (using her own pronunciation and a great deal of racy dialect which would have confounded the prophets); but, half-way through, her eye would light on a cutting and she would be off into a parable of her own, telling me the tale of some far-away picnic, or living over again the time when she sang "O Rowan Tree" at the church concert.

When I demanded "a story from the Bible", I was never sure whether I was to hear about the Burning Bush or the time when Uncle Andrew stopped the runaway horse; and it was many years before I could be sure which were Bible stories and which were family episodes. Indeed, I was under the impression for a long time that Uncle Andrew himself held his place among the prophets, and was surprised to discover that all Bibles didn't contain a recipe for marmalade in Deuteronomy.

When the minister called to see Granny she would inquire if he had chosen his text for the following Sunday, and if not would proceed to choose one for him and to give him his various "headings". He listened with commendable gravity, and, indeed, often accepted her advice (though not her phraseology), and doubtless his discourse was all the better for it. I, myself, was convinced that Granny was the better preacher of the two, for the minister stuck too closely to the Book for my liking, and had no "tales on the side" to tell of the speckled hen or the time the chimney went on fire.

When neighbours were in trouble and came to Granny for advice, she would always find consolation for them in the Bible, whether it was a comforting text or a "Remedy for the Toothache". Indeed, Granny's Bible came to be looked upon as a village encyclopaedia, to be consulted on a wide range of subjects, from the exact date of the Relief of Mafeking (which was noted down in spidery writing on a margin) to the best way of taking ink-stains out of a tablecloth.

"It's wonderful what ye'll find in the Bible," Granny would remark, peering over her spectacles and sucking contentedly at a peppermint. "Here's the story o' Noah; an', mercy me! here's a photo o' me as a lassie. Aye, it's a wonderful book, the Bible."

S.W.A.L.K.

by Robin Smyth

THE FIRST TIME I ever fell in love I was around eight years old, a London evacuee billeted in a lowland Scottish village.

She came upon me suddenly from behind a flowering bramble thicket which stood between Farmer Steven's cow-field and the black gravel path which led half-way to Gretna. She was blonde and pig-tailed, blue-eyed and dimpled, a tiny stranger in a Royal Stewart kilt and black patent shoes. She crouched in the spring sunshine, sucking her thumb and staring at me as I balanced dangerously on the thick lip of the rusty iron trough which stood near the hedgerow.

I stared back, enraptured, the way Adam must have done when he first encountered Eve. I tingled inside. It was a new and foreign feeling and it scared me a bit.

I think she experienced similar feelings because within half an hour we were pledged together in eternal love and I was sitting on the grass beside her, holding her hand and plucking up the courage to kiss her, when suddenly an adult voice, anxious and strident, came floating towards us on the wind.

"Moooooira. . . . Mooooooooira!"

The little girl jumped up and put one dimpled hand to her mouth and gasped, "It's my mither . . . we're awa' back tae Glasgow today."

And without another word she skipped away across the clover field and I never saw her again.

The war ended and I came back to London, back to the monstrous buildings which seemed to me as though they might topple down at any

D

moment, back to the concrete fields of Fulham and the tidy, friendly little street which stood sandwiched between the gigantic chimneys of Fulham Power Station and the sprawling, ugly Metal Polish factory, back home!

I had a broad Scottish accent and a hated kilt and a tasselled, leather sporran and all the little London boys whistled after me on buses until eventually I adamantly refused to budge from the house unless I were allowed to wear short trousers. With sentimental reservations, my mother stored the little patch of Gordon tartan and the tiny purse away in some dark, moth-balled cupboard . . . and I was happy.

But it's not so easy to store away a Scottish accent and it lingered with me for years. At primary school in Peterborough Road, the headmaster made me get up in the hall at the end of term and recite "To a Mouse" and "A Man's a Man for all That", in front of the whole, tough, ragged assembly. And I did, so unintelligibly that the enraptured audience must have thought me to be some wild, strange creature from beyond and applauded me to the echo.

From that day onwards, I was one of them. But they persisted in calling me Scottie.

Gradually the years wore on and by the time I was twelve I had lost all traces of my beautiful brogue and I was now a child of the streets. No more the green fields and the sturdy trees and the grey sea-shores of Scotland, but instead the asphalt roads and the muddy littered banks of the Thames by Carnwath Wharf where we dared our lives on oil-drum rafts. And in the evenings, on the low copings outside the squat, terraced houses, we would sit in the smoky twilight and play, "Truth, Dare, Promise, Kiss or Love", with the bashful, gym-slip girls.

There were a lot of little girls down our street, nice little girls, giggling little girls with ringlets and skipping ropes and glossy pictures of handsome film-stars tucked away in canvas school-bags.

And there were the boys, haring about on wooden, ball-bearing scooters and shooting marbles in the gutter and playing "Knock Down Ginger" on old ladies' door-knockers, violent, wiry, scruffy little boys with tender hearts, falling in and out of love with the rapidity and fickle-ness of buck-rabbits.

I, like the rest, fell in love regularly. It was like a ritual.

First there was the grubby love-letter, usually beginning: "My dearest, darling, most beautiful, delightful, so and so, I love you. Do you love me?", and invariably ending: "Please do not show this letter to anybody else. Please burn it." These letters were usually written, with great care, on a page ripped from a school exercise book and then they were elaborately sealed in a purloined envelope. Across the envelope were scrawled such romantic ciphers as: S.W.A.L.K. (Sealed with a loving kiss) and B.O.L.T.O.P. (Better on lips than on paper) and the envelope was then decorated with bleeding arrowed hearts and criss-cross kisses, and delivered by hand, usually by Mary Hannery, an earnest, fat, spotty girl, who never received such romantic missives herself and who seemed to gain a vicarious pleasure out of her role as the street's junior Cupid.

After sending such a letter, I would wait with some trepidation, playing five-stones or flickems up the wall for picture cards until Mary Hannery returned.

If Mary brought back a letter similar in content to the one I had sent, all the other boys would laugh and jeer and I would laugh with them as was the custom, then I would sneak off indoors to scrub my face and hands and to comb my hair and set it in high quiffs, and then off I would go to see my new amour.

I would usually find her at the far end of the street playing some gentle game with the other girls such as "King of the Golden River" or "Initials" and I would sit on a coping watching them and making corny remarks, and the object of my temporary affection would cast demure glances across at me and smile bashfully and all the other little girls would giggle knowingly.

At length I would jump up and join boisterously in the game, showing off like mad, until eventually I made some slight physical contact with my chosen girl, like pulling her hair or tripping her over . . . and then the romance was cemented.

Sometimes, however, Mary Hannery would return without a letter and instead she would deliver a curt verbal message with unconcealed enjoyment: "Jeannie Fulson says she 'ates the sight of you and would you kin'ly stop sending 'er soppy letters", or, "Margie Thomas says she loves Charlie 'Amilton what lives in Appleby Buildings and she wouldn't love you if you was the last person left on earth, so there!"

On such occasions I would vow to hate all women through Eternity—and my hate would last anywhere up to two days.

There was one particular girl I remember. Her name was Sylvia Russell, a blue-eyed blonde girl with the firm and splendid body of an adolescent Miss World. She reminded me greatly of that little girl Moira whom I had encountered so briefly in that wind-swept Scottish field several years before. I loved Sylvia to the point of distraction. She was lithe and athletic and she had the same quality of laughter that had so enthralled me with Moira. But Sylvia was a proud girl. Mysterious and womanly and unattainable, even at the tender age of twelve. Every boy in the street was after her, sending love letters, bearing tiny gifts, posturing and prancing and wrestling and racing in order to gain her attention. But Sylvia ignored us all with a cold indifference that at times was almost frightening.

I decided to improve my appearance in the hope of winning her favours. Night after night I would hang by my arms from my bedroom door desperately trying to increase my gnomish height. I wore a tight clothes peg on my nose to flatten the nostrils and succeeded only in bringing up two nasty, red sores. I scrubbed my teeth with salt and soot, and I rubbed my shoes until they gleamed like polished glass.

But she didn't even seem to notice me.

Now Sylvia had a sister who was a year older than she, a frail, pale-faced, wide-eyed child who used to sit at the front room window overlooking the street and gaze down at us lively, lucky kids as we danced and played and laughed and led our merry lives.

Nobody really took much notice of her. She was just "Iris-at-the-window". We all knew that she was an asthmatic but that didn't mean much to sparkling kids like us.

In the winter when the snow was on the ground, Iris would sit at the window wrapped in heavy blankets, her white face pressed against the frosty glass, watching us enviously as we built snowmen and hurled snowballs and rolled each other in the crisp snow. Often Sylvia would sit with her, and I knew that Sylvia loved her.

At the close of spring, when the sun grew warmer and the green leaves thickened on the eight plane trees which lined the left-hand side of the street, Iris would sit with the window open and sometimes we would hear her tiny rattling laughter as she watched us play. She seemed to get thinner and her eyes seemed to grow bigger and her skin paler as the days wore on.

More and more Sylvia would sit at the window with her, combing Iris's long, straight hair and fixing it up with blue and white ribbons, and now and then Sylvia would hug her sister tightly and smile at her.

Beautiful, smiling Sylvia, I worshipped her.

One day we were playing Releasio and the coping outside the Russells' house was our den. The boys had set off to capture the girls and bring them back to the den and I had elected myself den guardian, in the hope that I would see Sylvia and maybe talk to her as she sat at the window with Iris. I looked up at the window several times but neither Sylvia nor Iris appeared. I sat, unaccountably lonely in that empty street, and listened to the excited laughter of the running girls and the triumphant yells of the boys as they chased their quarry through the adjoining streets.

It was a warm, sultry day and I could see the heat shimmering from the tarmac road as I sat in the great black shadow cast by the biggest plane tree in the street which grew outside the Russells' house.

I sat for a moment, dreaming of Sylvia. Suddenly something hit me on the top of the head and bounced into the gutter. It was a small cob-nut. I frowned and rubbed my stinging scalp and gazed up into the leafy branches of the tree. Then I heard the girls giggling and I looked up at the window. Sylvia and Iris smiled down at me.

My heart bounced. I jumped up and stood on the coping and grinned at them. Iris giggled again and hid her mouth behind her bony hand and coughed hoarsely.

"Would yer like a cream sandwich, Scottie?" Sylvia invited me innocently. "A cream-cheese sandwich what I've just made?"

I rubbed my hands with over-done glee and chomped my lips. "Not 'alf," I said enthusiastically. "I'm starving." In fact I had not long since eaten a gigantic breakfast . . . but how could I say no to Sylvia?

Sylvia produced a thick, crusty sandwich and placed it on the window-sill. Iris spluttered with laughter.

"You'll 'ave to climb up and get it," said Sylvia. "I can't come down there. My Mum said I've gotter sit 'ere wiv Iris."

I needed no second bidding. I jumped off the coping and into the small concrete front garden and I shinned up the drain-pipe to the upper floor of the house. Gingerly I reached out for the concrete sill, gripped it with both hands and untwined my legs from the drain-pipe. I hung for a moment, then I heaved myself up and sat on the sill grinning at the two girls with triumph and egotism.

Sylvia looked at me disdainfully and Iris lowered her eyes trying to conceal her admiration. I sniffed. "Fanks!" I said and I picked up the chunky sandwich. It smelled scenty and soapy and I could see that the thick substance which oozed from the bread was creamy shaving soap out of a tube.

Sylvia gazed at me with undisturbed innocence as I raised the sandwich to my mouth. Iris looked slightly ashamed.

"Smells good," I said, and I took a huge bite at the creamy joke-sandwich. I chomped with mock eagerness and as the soapy substance swirled in my mouth I blew gently so that a crowd of little bubbles formed on my lips. I made suitably funny faces and ejaculations and pretended to fall off the window-sill, and Sylvia and Iris fell upon each other with laughter at the outcome of their practical joke.

And I was glad.

One day soon after this occasion, fat Mary Hannery came waddling up to me in the school playground with a note.

"Sylvia Russell asked me to give you this," she said.

I took the letter from her and looked at the envelope. It was smothered with kisses and hearts and romantic endearments and I nearly collapsed with joy.

I tore open the envelope and pulled out the carefully folded blue note-paper which was also smothered with criss-cross kisses, and I read it with hammering heart:

"My dearest, brave, handsome, wonderful, delightful, Scottie,
    I love you. Do you love me?
        Love and lots of kisses,
            Iris."

Iris? I was shattered . . . completely shattered. Poor, skinny little Iris . . . but I wanted Sylvia to love me . . . not Iris.

Mary Hannery was looking at me, biting her nails and fidgeting impatiently. "Come on," she moaned, " 'urry up. I ain't got all day."

"Just a minute," I said heavily, and I took out a pencil stump from my jacket and at the bottom of Iris's letter I wrote:

"Iris,
    I love someone else, I do not love you,
        Scottie."

I gave it to Mary Hannery to give to Sylvia and then I turned and ran miserably across the playground.

Iris Russell died when she was fifteen and from that day to this the window where she used to sit has remained empty. Now, as I look back over the happy, haunted years of my childhood, from the fields of Scotland to the tight, back-streets of Fulham, I often wish that I had written on that little note which Iris sent me:

"Dearest, darling, lovely, beautiful Iris,
    Yes, I do love you,
        Love and kisses,
            Scottie."

It might have made her happy . . . for a little while.

Instant Heirlooms

by Philip Holland

INSTANT IS A word we hear a lot nowadays—instant coffee, instant lather, instant cake-mix, even instant beer and now, according to the Personal Column of *The Times*, it's even possible to acquire an instant heirloom.

This is how the advertisement read: "Of interest to all Americans having British ancestry. Unique opportunity to acquire an exquisite handmade Limerick-lace christening robe and bonnet as family heirloom." Well I thought I knew what an heirloom was, but just to be on the safe side I looked it up in the dictionary. "Heirloom," it says, "—piece of personal property that has been in family for generations." Well, that seems clear enough.

Then how, you may ask, does it come about that you can now, apparently, turn somebody else's exquisite handmade Limerick-lace christening robe and bonnet into *your* family heirloom at the drop of a cheque? Ah, but you see this advertisement doesn't say that you can—at least not exactly. "Of interest to all Americans having British ancestry", it says. The advertiser has realized, you see, that there are hundreds of people in our American colonies who know nothing of their ancestry, poor fellows, except that it's British. There they are, these brave men and women of the frontier, cut off from home, with only the knowledge of their British blood to sustain them in their lonely struggle. Surely it's understandable that they should want, indeed need, some tangible link with home—an heirloom, so to speak, if not of their mother, then of their mother country.

Wait a minute though. I've just noticed—there's more to this advertisement. "The lace," it continues, "has historic interest, being once the property of an English queen, over a hundred years old and in perfect condition." The lace, that is, not the queen. I don't know how you are on history, but I can reckon up the number of English queens we had a hundred years ago on one finger. So why "an English queen"? Why not, in these frank and fearless days, come right out with it and say "once the property of Queen Victoria"? Surely this would make it an even more valuable heirloom for a Winnipasaukee family to acquire?

No, I'm afraid it wouldn't. Because, you see, the whole point of instant heirlooms is that they should be vague. It's all very well, when you're dandling your grandchild on your knee, to know that the exquisite Limerick-lace christening robe and bonnet that you're dandling him— or, of course, her—in, came (a) from the motherland, and (b) once belonged to a queen. But if you know that it belonged to a specific queen— to wit, Victoria—then at once you're in trouble. Just how, your neighbours will ask, are you related to her late majesty? You see the difficulty? Before you know where you are, you'll find yourself having to invent a family tree, and we all know the trouble that can get you into. By the time you've invented a lineage between yourself and the House of Hanover to cover the last hundred years, you'll be related to half the crowned—and ex-crowned—heads of Europe. The thing snowballs, you see.

It's just occurred to me, in fact, that what the present Limerick-lace christening robe and bonnet owner may be suggesting is not, in fact, that you should acquire an *instant* heirloom at all. But rather that you should, so to speak, lay one down, as fathers used to lay down cellars for their sons. I suppose all you'd have to do would be to tie the thing up in a parcel, mark it "Not to be opened till 2066", and put it in a bank vault. I'm sure your great-great-grandchildren would be delighted when they opened it. But I can't help thinking they'd be even more pleased if you made the thing yourself.

Bed-time Story

by John Ebdon

YOU KNOW LIFE is difficult. A few evenings ago, working on the theory that all experience is good for the soul and so on, I volunteered to do a spot of baby sitting, or to be more precise, child watching, and quite honestly I don't think I'm going to do any more. At least not without vetting the child first and making sure I get a nice simple-minded one of about five, because the other night I didn't. I got a nasty sophisticated one of about six. And it was quite dreadful. I'll tell you what happened. I went round to these people—they're out of the country at the moment by the way so it doesn't matter what I say—and after the usual skirmishes in the hall about "how good it was of me to come no it isn't I enjoy it really" sort of thing, I was led upstairs to its room, introduced, or rather re-introduced because we'd met briefly in the garden about a week before that, and left sitting in a cane chair three sizes too small for me and feeling rather like a stuffed owl.

I must say it was an attractive *looking* child, very pink and white and blonde and so on, but it didn't say anything. It just kept looking at me as if it expected me to turn into a pumpkin or something. And you know it's awfully demoralizing to be stared at like that—at least it is for me. Anyway, after about forty seconds of this brain-washing it broke its vows of silence and told me—it didn't ask, it told me—in a quiet authoritative voice to tell it a story.

I was so relieved at the slackening of tension that I suppose it went to my head. I told a story all about a beautiful princess who found a frog and how she took it to bed with her and how when she woke up she found it had turned into a handsome prince. You know the sort of thing; I think the original was written by some Balkan halfwit or other, but I added a few of my own touches to it. In fact I did more than that. I put everything I knew into it. I went falsetto for the princess, I produced a rich-handsome-prince type voice; and whenever the frog appeared I went, "Reeap"—no, it really was jolly good. And do you know what the beastly child said when I finished? It glowered at me over the coverlet and said, "I don't believe it," just like that; no word of thanks or anything, just "I don't believe it." So I said, "Well no, darling, I don't suppose you do but you're not supposed to. It's a fairy story." "Yes I know but it's a silly one because he'd wake her up." "Who would?" "The frog. When he was changing into a prince he'd make a noise as he was growing and she'd wake up and see him a bit of each and she'd scream and go mad and have to see Daddy." Daddy is a psychiatrist.

Well to cut a long story short, I was given a complete analysis of the whole situation, and frankly by the time Daddy came back I was ready to see him professionally. But of course the child was quite right. Unless the princess was either drugged or stone deaf she would have woken up. I mean you can't just change from a frog to a man without causing a bit of disturbance, can you? She'd be bound to collect a kick or two in the process. And then, as that little beast said, there'd be a pretty good chance of her seeing the chap in the half-way stage and frankly the mind boggles at the possible after effects, doesn't it?—magistrates' courts and goodness knows what. Anyway it's cured me of telling fairy stories to psychiatrists' daughters.

"The 14th Mr. Race"

by Steve Race

WHEN SIR ALEC DOUGLAS HOME became leader of his Party, some people made reference to the fact that he was the 14th Earl of Home. Sir Alec replied that just as he was the 14th Earl of Home, so was his opponent the 14th Mr. Wilson.

In other words it isn't only aristocrats who have ancestors: we all have. You, for instance. At the time of Waterloo there were probably about thirty direct ancestors of yours alive. Go back to 1649, and the day when Charles I was executed; about a thousand of your direct ancestors were living then. I don't suppose you're descended directly from Charles I, but it's quite possible that one of your great-great-great-great-great-great-grandfathers was present at the royal execution. And his grandfather could conceivably have sailed with Drake.

Now this sort of thought either does or doesn't excite you. Personally I find the romance of history so strong that I never bother to read a novel if I can be reading a biography. You know, somewhere in England in 1815 there must have been a man called Race, who stood in a crowd and cheered as the victory of Waterloo was announced. How exciting to know who he was and where he lived.

Well, thanks to a good deal of research, I *do* know. He was Joseph Race, a lead miner. He lived in a village called Hawkwellhead (only he would have called it Ha'kleheed) near St. John's Chapel in County Durham. He was twenty-three years old when a newspaper was brought down to the dale from Newcastle, a half-holiday declared, and Willy Gibson, who was educated, was called in to read aloud the victorious news. Joseph Race was courting a girl called Sarah Gibson. Two years later they married at the church six miles up the road. Their eldest son Joe was my great-grandfather.

Genealogical research is the most fascinating hobby I know. It's like an endless detective story, of which you yourself are the hero. If you're tempted to start on your own ancestry, let me give you a few hints—strictly as a fellow-amateur. There are professionals who will compile your family-tree for money, but why should they have all the fun?

The first thing to search is your own memory. Then elderly relatives may be able to add a few links; there might even be a family Bible. Memories can be false, though. . . . So can impressive-looking books. I can't remember how many books have told me that the surname "Race" is a corruption of the Welsh "Rees". It isn't at all, it's a Yorkshire name, and before that possibly Dutch.

All over Britain, churches keep Parish Registers of Births, Baptisms, Marriages and Deaths—sometimes in terrible condition, but they do keep them. Many local libraries have transcripts of these registers. Then there's Somerset House, though it isn't generally known that the records there only go back to the 1830s. One soon gets beyond that point, which is fortunate, because getting copies of these records can become expensive.

In compiling a family-tree, you work backwards. It's fatal to find an interesting (say) Elizabethan character who has your surname, and then try to trace him forward to a link with yourself. The chances of your being connected at all are thousands to one against, and it's all wasted effort.

As a matter of fact, famous names and famous families are the biggest trap of all. Some people begin research purely for snob reasons: they want to be connected with a "good" family, or prove their right to a coat of arms. Their reward is often an unpleasant discovery: an ominous blank on some old Birth Certificate under the heading, "Name of Father".

No, you've got to be honest, put down the good and the bad, and not jump even to the most tempting conclusions. Log everything, even if you discard 99% of it later on, and do stick to one surname at a time. Each new generation you complete in your backward search doubles the number of surnames in your tree. Take me. My name is Race; my parents were called Race and Hurley. Their parent's names were Race, Dawson, Hurley and Hewitt, and *their* parents, Race, Teesdale, Dawson, Tiniswood, Hurley, Padman, Hewitt, and Martin. You see? Already there are eight surnames, and I'm only back to my great-grandparents.

One of the surprising things you'll discover is how often even the humblest person's name is written down by themselves or by some official. My great-grandfather is an example. He was not an important man, but at birth he was registered; two months later he was baptized; his name appeared in school registers and every ten years in the national census; he married, registered five children and had each of them baptized; he was listed as a householder, a landowner, a postmaster, as a litigant, in a ship's passenger list, as a club member, a voter and a lay-preacher; he paid tax, signed receipts, wrote letters, kept a diary. He also made a will, witnessed his daughters' marriages and eventually he died and was buried. The local paper printed his obituary. He was a simple countryman, but for seventy-two years his name and his affairs were constantly being noted down. Many of those documents exist, one only has to find them.

Of course it's the finding that's the fun. I've stood in a churchyard up to my ankles in snow, rubbing frost off tombstones. I've sat for days in remote public libraries, copying thousands of entries from old registers. examined vellum deeds in freezing church vestries and in stifling Dickensian lawyers' offices. I've invoked the aid of charming vicars and dotty parsons. I found one bachelor clergyman trying desperately to get a fire going in a ruined vicarage that no self-respecting bat would live in. He didn't know it, but a stone cottage in his parish was called "Anthony House" after a Stuart ancestor of mine called Anthony Race.

Generation by generation you inch your way back, and your family-tree grows. Then suddenly . . . there's a blank wall. It happened to me. After reaching a dead stop in the Weardale parish records I came to the reluctant conclusion that one of my male ancestors must have been left under a gooseberry bush by the fairies for there was absolutely no trace of him, apart from his name on his son's Marriage Certificate.

62

On a hunch I drove south over the storm-swept Harthope Fell, and in a parish church there in Teesdale, preserved on parchment in a mildewed old chest, was the marriage entry I needed in order to link up a further five generations. That one discovery extended the jigsaw and led me back another 200 years. Standing there, in the cheerless vestry, I had the exciting (and for me almost mystical) experience of looking at the spidery words "John Race". It was the actual signature of my great-great-great-great-grandfather, written painstakingly in that same room on his wedding day in 1735—the year Doctor Johnson's dictionary was published.

Romantic? Yes, for me. And four centuries earlier, when a Yorkshireman called John Race leased some ground from a landlord in Beverley—that was in 1386—he can hardly have thought that the transaction would be unearthed twenty generations later by one Steve Race. I wonder if perhaps in twenty generations from now . . . Well, it's an idea, isn't it? Perhaps I'd better preserve this week's *Radio Times*.

Drama In The Cathedral

by Simona Pakenham

MY GRANDMOTHER ALWAYS travelled light. After living in a particular house for twenty years or more, she was able to pack her personal belongings into a suitcase which most people would find inadequate for a weekend away from home. Her houses have always been beautiful and full of carefully chosen antiques, mostly bought for a song, but she had no sentimental attachment to any of her possessions and would prefer to sell all she had and start again from scratch rather than be bothered with cumbersome luggage. I admired and envied her detachment from the tyranny of material objects, though it caused me a good deal of pain and heartache in my youth.

I learnt to hide my treasures by the time I was a schoolgirl, carrying them laboriously, at the end of each holiday, round to a friend's house. If I had not done so most of them would have been missing without explanation or apology the next time I went to Ginny's for a holiday. It took me a dozen years and some painful incidents before I learnt to protect myself.

Ginny was fairly tolerant of mess in the nursery so long as we stayed in one place. It was when a move was in the air that she became unscrupulous. We moved often, travelling about six times a year from Edinburgh to France and back again. It was a tedious journey with several changes and Ginny could not endure to be burdened with luggage. At these times my treasured books and toys were in serious danger.

Not long ago, on a visit to Edinburgh, I went to look again at St. Mary's Cathedral where I had been taken to the children's services on Sunday afternoons. As I stood in the aisle the most horrid drama of my infancy, which had long been forgotten in the mists of time, suddenly came back in frightful detail.

I was sent there one Sunday with Ginga my grandfather (Ginny had a perfect technique for keeping herself from the scene of trouble) taking my favourite toy, a three-foot-high donkey on wheels, which I led on a string, along with us. The whole proceeding aroused my suspicions from the first and I asked a number of questions as I stood enduring the twice-daily indignity of being buttonhooked into my gaiters. "Why must Neddy come to church?"

"It's a special service for toys. Neddy wouldn't like to miss it."

"Well, Teddy ought to come then. He's the most important of my toys."

"Teddy doesn't much like church!"

"He does. He's thinking of being a minister one day."

"There, you see. He doesn't need to go so much. It will do Neddy much more good. He's a bit of a heathen."

It seemed I was to have no choice in the matter and in the end the three of us set off through the wide streets, empty in their sabbath calm. Neddy's wheels made an irreligious tumult crossing the cobbles, causing my grandfather, who hated to be conspicuous, to cast furtive glances over his shoulder. The afternoon was drear and drizzly, a typical Edinburgh Sunday in early December.

To my surprise, the cathedral was indeed full of toys and their owners. Small boys in their Sunday kilts sat nursing wooden engines. Small girls dangled their buttoned shoes into the space below the pews, sitting beside well-dressed dolls and woolly animals. Nobody else seemed to have brought a toy as large as Neddy and I had to sit on the outside of our pew instead of my grandfather so that I could keep hold of his string while he stood conspicuously in the aisle beside me. A churchwarden leant over to say a word to Ginga. He noticed the donkey.

"How splendid! What a generous little girl!" he said, and patted my shoulder. This remark struck me as sinister.

The service went its ordinary, unintelligible way. There were the lessons; "All things bright and beautiful"; the usual prayers. We made the weekly request that all things should be ordered by God's governess. Then we all sat down and fidgeted into positions where we could think our thoughts in the maximum comfort while the parson spoke his "few words" to us. "Dear children", began the preacher, and I went off into my weekly Sunday school dream, on this occasion about the coming holiday in France and how the very next Sabbath I would be sitting in the choir stalls of our little Anglican church there. Suddenly the words of the address began to force themselves into my consciousness. "Kind and charitable children . . . More blessed to give than to receive . . . the joy that your sacrifice today will give to many a poor little child who has not your advantages and may never have had a toy to play with." An awful suspicion had begun to dawn.

E

"When the organ starts to play," the clergyman went on, "I want you all to come quietly into the aisle with your gifts and stand by the ends of your pews. The sidesmen will form you into a little procession and you will walk towards the altar steps where I will be waiting to receive you."

Full realization dawning at last, I precipitated myself into the middle of the aisle beside Neddy and clutched him to my bosom. This was interpreted by my neighbours as a truly Christian eagerness to be the first with my gift and a couple of churchwardens hurried forward to prevent my making a spectacle of myself.

"There now, no need to rush. All in good time."

But it was in the opposite direction to that of the altar that I was trying to stagger. I found my way blocked by an increasing crowd of virtuous infants all forming up between me and the west door in quiet and orderly ranks. Ginga took me by the back of my coat and swung me round. A Sunday school teacher detached my arms from Neddy, set him on the tiles and restored the string to my hand. Bewildered by the swiftness of it all, propelled forward by the procession of children which had begun to move towards the parson, I did not begin to yell until I had arrived about two yards from his feet. Then I made up for the delay. I stood stock still, lifted my face to heaven and let out a bellow of rage. The power of my lungs was considerable and I forced them with all my might so that my face went first red, then purple, as Ginga described later, and black darkness began to descend upon my eyes. My head spun. The pillars and stained glass windows whirled round me. The organ roared, presumably in an attempt to drown my lamentation. I remember no more until I was outside the church with somebody else's nannie and Ginga and a churchwarden, all of them fluttering round me in a frenzy of embarrassment. Of Neddy there was no sign.

As the blackness cleared and I began to get my breath I could hear my grandfather speaking. "Of course we *ought* to have explained to the child, but my wife would not have it. They are all off to France next week and she did not want to have to travel with so large and cumbersome an object as that toy. This service appeared to her as a solution to her problem. I was not allowed to have my say."

It was a long time before my grandfather could be persuaded to go to church with me again.

My Mother's Linen Cupboard

by Trude Dub

PERHAPS NOTHING MADE my mother appear so much "the lady of the house" as her linen cupboard.

I see her before me, tall, erect, imperious, selecting from the bundle of keys the one that would open (what to my childish eye always appeared) a mysterious world.

I don't know whether the wardrobe was really so huge—in the country of one's memory everything is so much bigger—but I remember shelves from the floor almost to the ceiling, fronted with hand-crocheted lace or hand-embroidered scallops, for Mother had several such sets. On the shelves, snow-white linen reposed in geometrically neat piles, each tied with a blue, satin ribbon.

In the days when my mother got married, a bride in my native Czechoslovakia had to have dozens of everything. Large featherbed-slips for the winter and embroidered eiderdown-covers for the summer, square lace-trimmed pillowcases, endless rows of sheets and table-cloths, and napkins and damask by the yard. We always had that in stock and no sooner was one lot of bed-linen made up from the store than new material was laid in. It was a magic cupboard, that never became empty.

Several shelves were filled with my parents' personal linen—huge nightdresses and night shirts, long under-pants and frilly drawers, staunch bodices and fine lawn petticoats, to tie around the waist.

The kitchen in those days was the province of the maid or the cook, the piano had always one or the other practising daughter seated in front, various corners of the home were occupied by children learning, or Father reading, or people visiting. There was a hive of activity all over the place —laughter and music and voices everywhere.

And Mother, who was such an integral part of our home, who was of its very fabric, who was laughter and tears and life—how completely different she looked when she stood in front of her linen closet. For that was her kingdom. She lived with us, she was of us everywhere else but here was a little corner all her own. Here she was herself.

I was always a bit afraid of her when I stole upon her unexpectedly, arranging her neat stacks and bundles, putting the new linen, fresh and crisply laundered to the bottom of the pile. I did not dare to ask her why she did it. I was conscious of watching some strange ritual, and I even didn't know whether she was aware of my presence. She was so withdrawn . . . so far away. . . . Sometimes she would put her hand right into the inner depths of the cupboard and withdraw a bundle of letters tied with a pink ribbon or an old album with photographs.

I used to feel angry. She did not have any right to have a life away from us. She was ours! "Mother," I used to cry, "wake up!" pulling frantically at her skirt.

She would then lift me up and kiss me and put away her memories and delve into another corner of the capacious linen-closet and bring out her heavily embroidered canvas rag-bag, with a silk cord threaded through bone rings. She would let me play with it and select some pieces for my dolls' dresses whilst she hastily put away the rest of the linen.

Many, many years have passed since then; the ever replenishing magic of the cupboard was halted and the secure world of the linen closet is no more. But I remember it still, with all its fragrance.

Sometimes when, hastily and impatiently, I am putting away my own linen, a whiff of that perfume teases my memory. It would be impossible to describe it, compounded as it was of fresh linen, lavender, pressed roses and something strange and elusive—the fragrance of my youth!

Touch

by Sheila Jefferiss [a blind listener]

My God, I thank thee very much
For all the lovely things I touch;
For velvet petals where I pass,
For clean, cold purity of glass;
For warm and welcome kiss of fur,
On gentle things who bark and purr;
For glow and glamour of all that sings,
When I caress a blackbird's wings;
I think the joys of Heaven are such,
That I shall know them all by touch.

HIGHDAYS AND HOLIDAYS

A Pleasure Of Picnics

by Agnes Ingle

SAMUEL PEPYS HAS given us the essence of a picnic. "A frolic took us," said he, "and off we went down the Thames with a bottle of wine, some cold meats, and cherries bought by the way, and we ate and sang in the boat." To me that's the stuff of picnics. The occasion, the place, the casual eating, combine to heighten your awareness of things. The very word brings to mind the murmur of the sea, or the hum of bees on a moorland, or the lap of water against a boat. The Oxford Dictionary says a picnic is "a pleasure party, including a meal out of doors", so putting the emphasis on the surroundings.

But of course, you begin on the eating level. When we sandwich-conditioned Britishers get on the Continent, there are pleasant surprises in store for us. I was once in a train in Italy which stopped for a time at Pisa. To most folk that word says "Leaning Tower". Not to me, however, for I often find that some kind of malign Fate seems to stop me from seeing the Proper Sights. So with Pisa. Not a vestige of that famous tower could I see, but what did catch my eye were lunches being sold on the station platform—in brown paper bags priced about 6/-. What was the Italian idea of a packed lunch? Well, in that bag were a cardboard dish of savoury macaroni, a cold chicken wing, a piece of cheese, two rolls, a couple of pears, and a bottle of wine, plus a small spoon, fork and cup. So, though I hesitate to say it, Pisa to me means packed lunch.

Some of the highlights of my picnicking experiences were during my inter-war residence in North China. Of course, for generations, Chinese pilgrims have toiled up to their hillside temples and shrines, but the sight of us with our bundles of food which we ate in the temple precincts or courtyards, where the priests would always bring us hot Chinese tea, was a constant source of wonder to the casual bystanders. One old man once asked me whether somebody paid us to carry our food up there to eat. To the average Chinese it was just one of those mysteries inseparable from "foreign devildom" which Confucius told them neither to consider nor discuss.

I remember a favourite temple in these hills, that of the Sleeping Buddha, a resort in ancient times of the Emperor Ch'ien Lung. We used to sit outside one special pavilion on a height, and look across the vast stretch of plain towards Peking. Immediately below was a lotus pool in the shade of an old ginko tree. Every now and then you glimpsed a saffron-robed monk gliding through a court-yard, or you could hear the beat of the bronze gong and the chanting of offices. More delightful still was the sound of the little bells which hung from the eaves of the pavilion roof and tinkled and clanked in the breeze.

Actually, you hadn't really picnicked in China if you hadn't gone in one of their fantastic house-boats on one of those stretches of water which seemed to have got enclosed within the walls of quite a few Chinese cities. The capital of Shantung, where I lived, had one called the "Ta Ming Hu"—the Lake of the Great Brightness, round which, on various islands, were temples, tea-houses, and small lotus farms. Lanes of reed-bordered water connected the larger tracts, and our big, lumbering boat, complete with table, chairs and glassed-in cabin was poled leisurely from one landing stage to another. This was exactly the sort of expedition you read about in Marco Polo and it was indeed a Prince of Picnics.

I call a picnic a kind of travel in miniature, for it has the feeling of limit-less time, and gives so many chances for friendly, casual contacts, which we are usually too aloof or too busy to find. In a foreign country, this is one way of learning about its people and their ways. One "old-China-hand" tells of how he was embarking on one of these boat picnics, and as he was paying off his rickshaw coolie, he felt sorry for him and gave him more than the agreed fare. At once the man set up the well-known clamour for more, following him right on to the boat. He was promptly bundled off by the "Lao Ta"—"Old Great," the boatman in charge. However "Old Great" delivered a lecture to the Englishman, then a "new-China-hand". "This is your fault," said he. "You agreed on the fare and then gave more. The coolie thinks you're a fool, who can't keep either his word or his money, and says to himself, 'He gives me more, he might as well make it more still'. So," ended the lecture, "stop giving more than is right, or you will have bad times in China."

But you don't need to go abroad to find on such picnic occasions the moment of—shall I call it truth, or exultation? I was once, with my husband, a keen botanist, eating a picnic lunch beside a pine wood on the shores of north-west Scotland. He was lamenting an unsuccessful search for a particular wild flower. Then, as our eyes roamed round, we suddenly saw, on a nearby rock, a white blob. It was this long looked-for "sundew". Examined in detail the perfection of its structure was breathtaking. Truly, here was something unplanned and unmakeable by us clever humans. God is in His heaven, even though all does not seem right with our world!

I think I can improve on the dictionary's definition. A picnic is a meal or a snack, eaten with light hearts, in happy fellowship, in a place somehow unforgettable.

New Clothes For Whit

by Winifred Howard

FOR THE KIDS at the Elementary School in the West Riding mill town in which I spent my childhood, Whitsuntide, thirty-odd years ago, meant new clothes, the Procession, and the races.

It really began in Sunday School weeks beforehand where we learned and practised hymns specially selected and printed in a new hymn sheet each year. For the girls—if you were lucky and the menfolk were not "playing", on short time, "laiking", layed off from work completely for a period, or "on Lloyd George", that is off sick—there were visits to the dressmaker, because at Whitsuntide you had your new clothes. The boys had a new suit, shirt, tie, socks and shoes. The girls had a new dress, coat, hat—a straw hat with flowers under or round the brim—socks— white socks with blue butterflies I remember one year—and shoes, shining black patent-leather shoes, with ankle straps too, if you really got your heart's desire.

On Whitsunday morning you were arrayed in your finery by your mother for the family to admire. "Keep your mouth shut tight while I pull the dress over your head." "Don't put owt in your pockets. It'll mak' 'em bulge." "Don't dirty your socks."

With the last "don't" ringing in our ears—"Don't take owt from your Auntie Emma, she can't afford it,"—we were sent to display ourselves to neighbours and relatives. There squealing but smiling, we had to suffer the traditional pinch or "nip for new clothes" and receive gladly, if with a little embarrassment, the coppers bestowed on us to jingle in our pockets.

Clothes were changed for Sunday dinner. We had one cup of water on the table to pass round. Why only one? I've never found the answer to that. "Stand still and eat your dinner", echoes down the years, not "sit still" but "stand still". I'd forgotten that. There were six of us in our family. The older ones came in at different times on weekdays so Sunday at mid-day was the only time we all had a meal together, and then there weren't enough chairs for us all to sit at the table.

After lunch we changed back into our new clothes and went off to church. No Sunday School on Whitsunday but a special service in the afternoon with the full choir and a roof-raising rendering of the well-practised hymns.

Then home to tea where we had hard-boiled eggs with the yolk scooped out, mixed with sardines and put back again; home-made cakes and perhaps special shop-bought marzipan-topped cakes as a treat if there were visitors, and a whispered admonition "Mind you don't ask for more than one."

But Whitmonday was really *the* day. After mid-day dinner we all met at the church, and we youngsters were proud if we had an elder brother in the choir to wear a cassock. There was a short service, a hymn to get us going, and then we went out into the road to form up as a procession outside the church gates. The vicar, the gleaming cross and the church banners were at the front, the choir and congregation behind, and at the end two or three decorated and garlanded open lorries with chairs on for the youngest children and the elderly.

Round the parish streets we went all afternoon, stopping at various vantage points to sing a few hymns and take a collection—Cullingworth Street and the hospital, outside the Park gates and at the top of Pildacre Hill, and, of course, at the Workhouse.

The singing did at last come to an end and on to the Sunday School we went for tea—currant buns, cakes and lemonade. A rest followed and then on again to the Field. The Field usually belonged to some farmer and one hoped not too many cows had been using it beforehand for, if they had, it was none too easy to find somewhere to sit.

In the Field there were, first of all, races to be won: egg and spoon, sack, three-legged, wheelbarrow, blindfold and plain running. There were shouting and cheering and laughter, and among the prizes coveted shining, smooth, bouncy, coloured balls of all sizes. When the races were over and the prizes distributed, the brass band arrived complete with gold braid, flat-peaked caps and great gleaming instruments booming "oom-pah-pah" all the way round the field. From then on we sang and we danced, in between maybe eating a ha'penny ice cream cornet, until dusk hid the gaunt mill chimneys in the valley and brought another Whitsuntide to an end.

Buckingham Palace Garden Party

by Jack Singleton

MORNING DRESS OR lounge suit—that was the question. A grey topper, striped pants and tails are all right if you're used to them—like a character in an Osbert Lancaster or Anton cartoon—but I'm not, so I gave my best suit an extra press and joined one of the queues outside the gates of Buckingham Palace—the Palace of Pimlico, as somebody once called it. It was a bit like getting into Chelsea at a cup-tie, as about ten thousand are invited and seven or eight thousand usually turn up. Anyhow, we went through two by two, ark-fashion, and crossed the fore-court, where the scarlet-coated guards keep watch. Sightseers crammed the railings, staring at us just as we were later to stare at the

Royals—only they are used to being stared at. We passed through Victoria's East Wing and across the quadrangle to the Grand Entrance of Nash's building. I handed in my ticket, then trotted up the stairs with portraits and pillars and branching corridors, to the beautiful Bow Room, so-called because of its many bow windows. A red carpet led to the terrace at the back, and to a whole new world most of us had never seen before.

Steps led down to a huge lawn, as smooth and green as a butler's apron, and a prospect of trees and paths and urns and flowers and lakes, over forty acres of intimate parkland. From the top of a bus, I'd had glimpses of it over the high spiked garden wall, but never imagined it so spacious. Apart from a faint hum of traffic, and of course the skyscraping Hilton Hotel, which has made all private space public within a square mile, I might have been at Windsor or Osborne or Sandringham. Two bands were sitting either side of the lawn, the Grenadier Guards and the Royal Marines. They took it in turns to play and ran up a flag when they were in session. Down one edge was the long tea-tent for the likes of me, and on the other, two pavilions, one for the Royal Party and the other for the Corps Diplomatique.

As it was only a quarter past three, and our hostess was not due until about four, I strolled round the grounds. On the Constitution Hill side was a path bordered by a bank of blazing flowers, and there was a rose garden, but it was the variety of trees and shrubs that impressed me most. In one grove was a large round summer house, full of children's toys. Prince Andrew's sand-pit had been covered up for the day. Nearby I inspected a tiny caravan with everything made to scale, the modern Wendy-house. From the branch of a plane tree planted by Princess Mary in 1913, I think the plaque said, two climbing ropes hung down for young aspirants to father's award.

The lake soon attracted me—part of the old Tyburn brook—winding between the trees and crossed by rustic bridges. On one bank were some huge metal storks, Giacometti fashion, and I watched some dab chicks scampering over the lily pads. Then my eyes were caught by a pink

79

peachy haze, almost iridescent, through some willow branches. I went along and there, in the heart of London, were several stately, grotesque, yet utterly beautiful flamingoes, with their question-mark necks and ramrod legs. In the winter, someone said, they migrate to warmer waters at the Zoo.

Through all this "rus in urbe" meandered a multitude of guests in little groups. Mayoral chains heaved on substantial corporations, hands kept clutching at unaccustomed top hats, uniform of every description preened itself. There were bishops in their gaiters, Africans in flowing cotton wraps, Indians in white Gandhi caps and black coats or in silken saris. Some Middle East gentlemen with tea-cloth headgear might have come straight out of *The Road to Zanzibar*, and, most fragilely lovely of all, there were the doll-like Japanese in embroidered kimonos and obis, escorted, of course, by their menfolk in full West End fig. Then there were all the other Garden Party ladies, wives, matrons, daughters, capitalizing the occasion to acquire new dresses, hats, and accessories of every shape and hue. Heaven forfend I try to describe them.

At four o'clock the Royal Party appeared on the terrace, and the National Anthem was played. The Queen was followed by Prince Philip, the Duke and Duchess of Gloucester, Princess Alexandra and ladies-in-waiting and gentlemen-at-arms. A few people were drawn up and presented, none, I noted, wearing morning dress. On the big lawn, the rest of us formed lanes, informally marshalled by the red and yellow Yeoman of the Guard with their halbards, and when the Queen and Prince Philip came down the steps Her Majesty took one lane and the Duke of Edinburgh the other. The Queen was dressed in a flowery hat, greenish dress, with a pink bell-shape coat, white shoes, gloves and bag. As she strolled along representative subjects were brought forward and introduced to her, and she stood and chatted, with the Lord Chamberlain, topper in hand, hovering a yard or two away, for all the world looking like an adjutant stork. About five yards behind, ladies-in-waiting and gentlemen-at-arms made a protective line which moved down the lane as the Queen advanced. You could usually tell where the Prince was by the laughter that followed in his wake. Incidentally, I'd never noticed before what large seaman's nostrils he has.

This was really the heart of the matter—the Queen and her husband meeting different members of their large family in as informal a manner as possible. There was dignity and homeliness. What followed—the rush for a cup of tea and a plate of bridge-rolls and cream cakes—counts for nothing. Her Majesty, I felt, had really been at Home This Afternoon.

Zeppelin Joy Ride

---

by Charles F. Resting

FROM WIMBLEDON COMMON I saw the first Zeppelin brought down in flames near Cuffley, Herts., on the night of September 3, 1916. For us it was a cheerful victory, but an awesome spectacle just the same. Eventually many others met the same fate, and it soon became obvious these easy-target monsters of the skies were utterly useless in modern warfare.

It was not until the late 20's that Zeppelins became front-page news again. Trips round Europe had for years been commonplace, but lately they had conquered new territory by frequent flights across the Atlantic, a trip to the Far East and Japan, and even a rescue operation near the North Pole.

War-time failure had apparently been turned into peace-time success.

F

An early summer day in 1932, I spotted a notice that the Graf Zeppelin would visit London and take a limited number of passengers for a trip round Britain. I phoned Cook's asking them to try and book me a passage. An hour afterwards I fetched the ticket, £42, plus insurance £6. It was a lot of money in those days for a week-end jaunt, but I was dying to go and quite prepared to cancel my annual holiday to balance my budget.

Hanworth Air Park near Staines in Middlesex was the starting point, and we had to be there by four o'clock Saturday afternoon, July 2. A crowd of some 25,000 had gathered to watch the Zeppelin and enjoy the fun. At 6 p.m. the commotion began—and there she was—just a tiny cigar, miraculously suspended in mid-air over the distant hills. Twenty minutes later she passed above like some awakened giant, dropped her landing gear by parachute, and shortly afterwards she found herself well and truly caught and moored by the 250 Volunteer Ground Crew.

The twenty-two passengers were collected and taken to the cabin-gondola. Mounted police pushed the crowd back, final megaphone instructions were issued, a bell tinkled, the five 562 horse power engines roared into life, and the sunlit airship floated gracefully away.

After some ten minutes' steep climbing, she levelled off and slowly nosed her way over prettily hedged Surrey and Hampshire. Glancing down on the fascinating kaleidoscope of the ever changing toy-town countryside, any initial fears I might have had soon vanished, and gave way to an exhilarating mixture of comfort, safety and high adventure.

An hour later we were over Portsmouth as a unique visitor on the opening day of the new airport. Numerous planes buzzed around in greeting and thousands waved from the ground. A final sweep, and in the rapidly greying evening sky, we headed inland again towards the Metropolis.

Now came the welcome sound of the dinner-gong, and at small separate tables we were served a meal that would have done credit to the best maître d'hôtel in London or Paris—caviare, lobster patties, roast joint, strawberries and cream, biscuits and cheese, coffee and liqueurs, vintage champagne. Delicious!

On top of that we had a fascinating show unmatched by the costliest cabaret in Town. London—dear old London—right below us, in all its charm and glittering finery. All the great arteries could be picked out with ease, and so low were we cruising that some swore they could read the electric signs in Piccadilly Circus.

And so out into the dark—Ipswich, Yarmouth and across the Wash, while we settled down in the cosy saloon for a quiet game of cards or getting-to-know-you chat.

The telegraphist offered to send wireless greetings to earthbound friends and relatives. "The cost please?" I asked. "One and twopence, Sir." It seemed amazingly cheap. So I got busy, and handed in seven long descriptive messages. He looked a bit surprised.

A final nightcap—and I went to bed about midnight—a bed as comfortable and free from motion as you could wish. It was like sleeping on a cloud.

I woke at four, dressed quickly, and with Berwick-on-Tweed below enjoyed a glorious sunrise over the North Sea. An hour afterwards, we circled the beautiful city of Edinburgh and the Forth Bridge. Glasgow was a more sombre sight with a close view of the giant, partly constructed *Queen Mary*, patiently awaiting better times for completion.

While enjoying a splendid breakfast we followed the Clyde to the open sea, passing the Isle of Arran and getting a peep at the Irish coast beyond. But fine weather now deserted us. Sea mist enveloped us completely when nearing the Isle of Man. The Zeppelin fired depth-shots repeatedly to ascertain our height. It felt very eerie and progress was dead slow.

We changed our schedule and headed for the Lancashire coast, making a sudden roll as we neared Liverpool at noon. Hooting Mersey steamers and ferry-boats greeted us. Looking down on Port Sunlight was exceptionally interesting to one of our distinguished passengers—Lord Leverhulme. And it gave me an idea!

I sought out the Commander in the navigation room. "Please, Dr. Eckener," I begged, "if we go anywhere near Birmingham, could we pass over Solihull where I live?" We could.

This was for me the totally unexpected high-spot of the trip. I saw my friends playing golf down there, where I would normally have been this time of a Sunday morning, and we cruised so low I easily picked out my very house and garden, with poor old Rover racing round like a maniac. I was thrilled.

A scrumptious lunch followed while we journeyed on to Cardiff and the south coast.

To stretch my legs I happily joined a conducted tour of the great dirigible—up through narrow hatchways and along the centre catwalk. This was a phenomenal length and took us nearly ten minutes steady crawling to get to the tail. We had to turn round all together. One false step, and not even a lifebelt could save you. Here were the quarters of the crew of twenty-four—just hammocks slung between girders inside the frail octopus. What a life, I thought, I hope they don't quarrel or sleep-walk! Back in the gondola we passed over the crowded beaches of sun-baked Bournemouth and the mammoth liners at Southampton.

We had a final get-together in the main lounge for a dainty tea. The wireless-operator presented his compliments—and accounts.

"What's this? £8 10s. 6d.? For me? Something wrong here," I said to him. "You said one and twopence last night, and I only sent seven messages."

"One and twopence—*per word*, Sir!"

How everyone roared with laughter, whilst I blushed like a schoolboy caught stealing granny's apples. I borrowed the money from a fellow-traveller and paid up.

We were now nearing Hanworth and the end of the journey.

Skilfully the Graf Zeppelin dodged the welcome-back reception from swooping planes of every size and description. The huge bulk dipped slowly—engines were reversed—mooring ropes were released—and the great ship made a perfect landing at 6 p.m. after a magnificent journey of some 1,400 miles—a week-end to remember!

Holiday Bonuses

by E. R. B. Reynolds

WHEN WE GO on our holidays, especially if we go abroad, we reckon that we are going to see some splendid things—this or that cathedral, this great gallery, that grand house and so on. But I've come to realize that apart from these special things which we "went to see", there are what I think of as the bonuses—the things which came upon us unexpectedly, took us completely by surprise and overcame us with delight. Let me tell you some of my bonuses on a recent holiday.

The first is utterly trivial. We flew over on the car ferry to Cherbourg and got there about midday. We drove, nice and steadily on the right, for half an hour and then stopped by the roadside for a picnic lunch. Along came a farm cart and as he passed the man in it waved his hand and called out "Bon appetit"—and we knew we were there! I could have blessed him. Why don't we say "Good appetite", or something in England?

Next—a splendid bonus. We got to Angers and made our way to the castle—a huge fortification which would impress anyone. We went in, four of us, and my heart sank when I had to fork out two shillings each. One of these French soak-the-foreigner rackets I thought. Apparently there were some tapestries to be seen and I've always hated tapestries; great clumsy, blown-up versions of pictures by Raphael or somebody, faded and worn and dreary. Why do the French seem to be so proud of the wretched things? Anyway, we'd paid up so we plodded across to the room and there they were. The first real tapestries I'd ever seen, beautifully exhibited in a vast L-shaped room, with lovely colours, mostly blues and pinks, and the most enchanting subjects—based on the Revelation of St.

John. They were full of the most vivid imagery: glorious seven-headed beasts, splendid angels, towers and castles, devils, monsters, saints and sinners, dragons and delectable trees and flowers, fiery furnaces—the lot. All were *meant* to be tapestries, they couldn't have been anything else, done round about 1400, I think. I know now they are world-famous, that I was a fool not to have made a special journey to see them (as many do), but for me they were a bonus, a completely unexpected joy.

Another bonus was at Fontevrault. We drove up into a very small place and my chief thought was that I'd have a job getting out again. Nearby was a locked gateway to an Abbaye, but it appeared to be, and in fact was, a large gendarmerie. Inside we were made to pay another two shillings apiece, and this time I was sure we'd been swindled. We were guided past a row of once-elegant houses where the gendarmes were to be seen with their feet up on the tables, and came to a very large, very old kitchen, rather like the Abbot's kitchen at Glastonbury but larger and much more elaborate. It was interesting, but not eight bobs' worth. Next we saw a refectory where the prisoners fed—yes, it was a prison as well as a gendarmerie—the French make use of their Abbayes! By this time I was feeling definitely morose.

Then we came to a chapel which was entirely empty. I glanced at the windows and wondered what the old royal arms of England were doing there. The party moved along the nave, and all of a sudden, I knew. There was the bonus.

Four splendid recumbent stone figures—Henry II, Richard I, Eleanor of Aquitaine (Henry's Queen) and I've forgotten the fourth. *Our* kings and one of them Richard Coeur de Lion! The guide drooled on, the French looked bored and smelt garlicky and I wanted to shout out "Hey, let me tell them, they were *our* kings and one of them was Richard the Lion-hearted, the noblest of the lot." But I couldn't speak the language well enough and my wife would have died of shame if I had tried, so I just had to glow with joy and pleasure. Slap in the middle of France, mind you, and *our* kings. Of course I know now, because I've read it up, how they came to be there, I know that Richard I was a shocking king of

England—hardly ever set foot in it as king—and I know that he and his father Henry II were at daggers drawn. But all that doesn't matter. The sight of them was a splendid bonus, utterly unexpected and wholly exciting, and I shall never forget them.

The next bonus was an odd one. We stopped at a village called Carennac where the road ran close to the river and some thirty or forty feet above it. As we stopped we saw a small boy of about eleven and as we walked towards a nearby church which looked interesting, he joined us and asked us shyly if we wanted a guide. Another little racketeer? It could be, but he looked a nice child and anyway we said "Yes". What a bonus! He took us all over the church and the adjoining ruins, explaining everything clearly and lucidly. He praised the tympanum, enthused over a sixteenth-century Deposition in the church, told us which parts were Romanesque, which Gothic, and pointed out all sorts of interesting details of pillars and windows and such like. He was very flea-bitten, literally, and scratched himself absent-mindedly from time to time. We were all enchanted with him and marvelled that so small a boy could have mastered, or even have wanted to master, so much detail about his village church.

At the end I asked in my best French if it was permitted to give the guide a tip and he hastily assured me, "Ce n'est pas obligatoire." Obligatory or not, I got him to accept something. Then he shyly produced from inside his shirt a pamphlet and explained that all he had told us was in the pamphlet which we could buy, if we wanted to, in the church. It came out that he didn't live there at all but came from Dunkirk and was just on holiday with some relations in the village. An enchanting child and a splendid bonus—and we all came away feeling that Carennac was one of the nicest places we had seen. In fact, we wondered if we should offer to take him for a run in the car, but as he would certainly have left us a liberal legacy of fleas, we funked it and shook hands gravely instead.

I almost hesitate to mention the next two bonuses but they were such perfect examples of what I mean by the expression, that I must. We generally ate a picnic lunch except on Sunday—bread and cheese and paste and fruit—and after it I lit my pipe and strolled around looking for flowers we don't get in England. I found many orchids such as we get at home on the Downs but much, much bigger. One day, strolling along a hedge, I was startled, almost frightened, to see the most splendid orchid I've ever seen in my life. It was about thirty inches high, the flower part being about half that length and two inches or more wide. The separate florets, if that is the word, were rather like tiny lizards hanging tail downward, and the colours were like those swagger orchids you see in shops—brownish, yellowish, greenish. I hastily cut it and then had a guilty feeling that I shouldn't have done; maybe it was a great rarity. However I'd done it so I took it in triumph to the others who were as thrilled as I was. We took a colour photograph of it and I have since found out that it was a lizard orchid—not all that uncommon, but I have never been so excited by a flower in my life; for me it was a major discovery and I shall never think of that holiday without thinking of that flower.

And the last bonus? It was a purple Emperor butterfly, very hard to find in England—I've never seen one for sure, only wondered if *that* was one high in an oak-wood. This one was sunning itself on the ground and as I approached it, hardly believing my eyes, it fluttered on to a branch of a shrub two feet from my face. It opened and closed its wings a few times so that I could be absolutely sure of what it was and could admire the lovely purple sheen on its wings and before it flew lazily away. Shall I ever see another? I doubt it, but I shall never forget this one and I'm afraid I shall swank about it more than I shall about all the grand cathedrals and chateaux—but not more than the lizard orchid.

"Ern Per"

by Victor Lucas

IT WAS COLD in Paris that first week in January. There was ice in the Seine and a biting wind stirred the discarded tickets littering the steps leading down to the Metro. The city seemed half empty. No self-conscious Britishers wandered aimlessly along the boulevards in search of "Gay Paree", and the strip clubs around Place Blanche were finding it hard to make an honest living. Paris in winter contains only the French . . . the most hard-headed realists in Europe.

I had been filming at the Gare du Nord since eight o'clock in the morning, my feet frozen solid to the platform. After lunch, shooting finished for the day, I remembered hearing that the warmest place in Paris on a cold wintry afternoon is the Conciergerie on the Ile de la Cité, and it was not so much in search of the past as in need of warmth that I visited the subterranean Museum of the Terror, where during the French Revolution the doomed aristocrats had awaited transportation to the guillotine.

The Conciergerie was dimly lit and a pleasant musty smell of old stone hung in the air. After the cold outside it was like finding a place of sanctuary. My ears, which had been feeling as if they had bulldog clips attached to them, slowly began to thaw.

Behind a desk, guarding postcard reproductions, sat a world-weary French lady, unsmiling in black bombazine. In return for one new franc she issued me with a ticket, at the same time drawing my attention to a notice which read "ENGLISH SPEAKING GUIDE PROVIDED". The wooden barrier, beyond which lay the cavernous interior of the prison, was firmly

89

closed, and on it hung another notice stating that unaccompanied entry was forbidden.

My French is ungrammatical but resourceful and I asked if I might not be permitted to wander through the building alone, pointing out that the historic associations of the Conciergerie were celebrated and that its unique atmosphere spoke eloquently to those with the imagination to recreate the past for themselves.

Coldly, I was informed that this was strictly prohibited by the regulations. The guide himself, in his peaked cap, a man with no illusions about life, eyed me with disapproval.

Custom was far from brisk that afternoon, and I was asked to await further arrivals before a conducted tour could begin. Kicking my heels aimlessly, I began to feel something of an intruder.

"You are allowed to smoke while waiting," said the guide, in English, his hand already assuming that conformation of the fingers which precedes the withdrawal of a King Size from someone else's proffered packet.

"I don't smoke," I said. "Sorry."

"Quelle chance!" he muttered in disgust, his eyelids drooping even more than usual. Reluctantly, he produced a half-smoked Gauloise from behind his ear.

"Every things are very expensive in Paris," he said. "It costs very dear the cigarettes . . ."

Lighting the stub, he inhaled almost the whole of it in one long devouring draw. The smoke disappeared into his lungs and never came up again.

Time passed. After a while there arrived a German girl student with pebble lens spectacles and a black leather coat. Then ten minutes later, descending the steps from the street, came a family of four . . . Mother, Father, and two young boys.

The newcomers were British . . . as British as Bath buns or Brighton rock. Nice people, South London surburban, all of them a bit undersized; they looked around them uncertainly, talking in whispers as if to give each other reassurance in an alien land.

Father was hesitant but gently firm, Mother was pretty and unassertive.

The two boys (one aged about twelve, the other a few years younger) were wearing their school uniforms . . . secondary modern and primary respectively. They looked neat and well-mannered in their school macs, their navy blue and crested caps, and short trousers above knobbly knees. Their grey school socks had coloured stripes where the tops rolled over the knotted elastic.

What on earth, I wondered, was this family doing in freezing Paris in the first week of January, looking so vulnerable, so isolated from all that Paris is supposed to stand for, as out of place as Patagonians in Budleigh Salterton.

Buying the tickets, Father examined a five franc piece with cautious deliberation, not parting with it until he had established its face value beyond all reasonable doubt. He obviously felt this to be a necessary precaution in a country where the coinage was bewilderingly divided into the old and the new, and one could all too easily pay seven and ten-pence for a box of matches, or (worse contingency) offer a waiter a tip of the hundredth part of one and sevenpence.

The guide was speaking to me.

"Je sais que vous comprenez bien le français."

I nodded in qualified agreement, mentally deploying reserves of irregular verbs.

"Et vous, Mademoiselle?"

The lady from West Berlin obliged with a fluent assent in French of Teutonic precision.

He addressed himself next to la famille Anglaise.

"Et vous? Vous aussi? Hein?"

Father was a little out of his depth already.

"Pardon," he said humbly, in a low tone as if asking forgiveness for having made a rude noise.

The guide breathed out sharply through his nose and repeated the question testily. Perhaps his corns were troubling him and he just wasn't in the mood to be an English speaking cicerone that afternoon.

Father looked at him apologetically. The atmosphere was, as they say, tense. The honour of the Old Country was at stake as the waiting silence lengthened to all of eight seconds. They were a devoted and close-knit family, with a kindly concern for each other in terms of human dignity. Finally, Father spoke.

"Wee," he said. "Ern per."

The guide regarded Father stonily for a moment and then he abruptly opened the barrier and motioned for us to follow him.

As he conducted us through the building, he rattled through a prepared commentary in monotone French. I was getting about one word in four and following the gist largely by guesswork. At one point he described how the women would spend their last hours attending to their coiffure, the night before the tumbrils came to fetch them. The younger boy turned to his father.

"What did he say, Dad?" he asked in a trusting tone as to an oracle.

"Well, I didn't catch it all, David, but he was telling us about how the men used to pass the time playing cards."

As they lingered to study a case of exhibits I took the guide on one side and asked if he'd mind giving them a brief re-cap in English. He called to them with bad grace.

"Vous avez compris ce que je vous ai dit?" he demanded.

Father looked at him. Mother and the boys looked at Father.

"Ern per," said Father again, and in the heavy underground silence which followed you could hear his brain ticking over like mad in an unsuccessful and agonized attempt to phrase a further remark. There were beads of sweat on his forehead.

The guide moved away and continued his monologue in French.

Five minutes later, the tour completed, we arrived back at the entrance hall. The guide waited expectantly by the check point. Seeing the German girl tipping him, Father produced a handful of coins from his pocket. He spoke to me in a worried undertone, the money in his hand, his family hovering anxiously behind him.

"Excuse me. How much do you think I should . . ."

"This one," I said, separating one dull lightweight coin from the others

92

and holding it up between thumb and forefinger. He peered at it in the dim light and for a moment he looked startled. Then he smiled, and his eyes twinkled as they met mine. It was like the sun coming out.

Shepherding his wife and sons through the barrier, he placed slightly less than a farthing in the palm of the English speaking guide.

"Pourboire," he said. "Ern per."

Funny Things in Foreign Parts

by Basil Boothroyd

I SUPPOSE I'VE got a drawerful of the most undistinguished souvenirs in the history of foreign travel. Still, they're highly evocative for me. There's a marble chip from the Parthenon, for instance. This evokes the hottest day I ever remember, even in Greece. I was at the bottom of the Acropolis, wondering if I could ever climb up all those broken steps and live to tell the tale, when I saw a man selling ice creams, which seemed like a gift from the gods. So I pointed to one, in Greek, and he handed it over . . . and of course you can't trust those Greek gods, because it turned out that they weren't ice creams at all, but cones full of extremely thin and volatile honey that ran straight up your sleeve and down inside your shirt. That's how I picked up the marble chip. It's highly illegal to take away bits of the Parthenon—well, naturally, if everybody did, there wouldn't *be* one—but as I found this particular chip stuck to my shorts when I got in the taxi, it seemed to make it all right. I suppose it's only my imagination, but it still seems a bit sticky even now.

Or what about this frightening little tube of airline mustard? It reminds me of the only time I ever flew the Atlantic. It was in winter, and we had to go miles off-course to avoid a hurricane or something and messages kept coming over the loudspeakers about the fuel situation and whether we should have to put down in Boston, if we could get as far as Boston. I'm never at my calmest in aeroplanes, and when the Captain came through I asked him how things were going and he said he didn't know. And *I* said, hoping for something a bit more reassuring, "Oh, but I expect you're always having to cope with these problems." And he said, "Not like this one," and passed on. It was then I found I'd been trying to light a cigarette with this tube of mustard.

A lot of these things seem to be souvenirs of cruises, and they chiefly remind me of the sort of people you find yourself on cruises *with*. They're much more sensible and conscientious than I am, when it comes to souvenirs. I don't know whether you've ever been on a cruise, but every time the ship puts in at some romantic spot, where you can see Christopher Columbus's rocking-chair, or the bones of a prophet, or something of that kind, hundreds of passengers go fighting down the gang-plank, yelling "Which way to the shops?" and brandishing their traveller's cheques; and a couple of hours later they come back with arms full of chiming clocks and Scotch whisky and other typical native products. No, it's perfectly true. I once saw a man come aboard from Naples with a home-knitting machine, made in Nottingham.

I was going to say that I hardly ever *buy* anything on these trips, but that isn't strictly true, because when I open this drawer the first thing that strikes me is a little tooled-leather notecase, just too small to take notes of any kind, for some reason. It strikes me first because of the smell, which is extremely pungent. I bought it in Lisbon, and I think it's a bit of Portuguese goat-hide that got made into a notecase before it was quite ready. My wife and I were trailing along at the back of a guided tour from the ship— I think we were being taken round a fish-packing plant—and this very old fierce man, with glittering eyes and a claw full of these horrible wallets, suddenly appeared and cut me off from the rest of the party. Very menacing, he was. I didn't want a wallet, let alone a wallet that nothing would go in, but I was terrified the party would move on and I should be lost in Lisbon. I'm always afraid this may happen, because I get lost very easily, even in places like Reigate or Leatherhead, where they have English-speaking policemen. So I bought the thing and ran. I didn't notice the smell at the time. I suppose because of the fish-factory.

But what it actually reminds me of is an enemy I made on that particular cruise. She was a very intense lady from Leicester, with a sharp nose and a sort of darting look, and to recall her clearly I also have to look at another souvenir of mine from the same ship, and I bet no one else in the world has got one. It's an X-ray photograph of my left foot, and when I get that and the note-case together the whole affair comes as sharp as a knife. It's got two instalments. First, I was standing on the edge of the ship's swimming pool, with no intention whatever of swimming. I wasn't even dressed for it. She was having her photograph taken, and she backed into me and knocked me in. Then she lost her balance and fell in on top of me. I kicked out for dear life, and broke my little toe on the side of the pool. She took the view that it was all my fault, for some reason.

Then—second instalment—about a week later we were all involved in one of those ship's parlour games, sort of floating quiz, and by a bit of bad luck our table was next to hers. This wouldn't have mattered, but the rules were that when the answers were read out by the Purser, each table marked the next table's papers, you see? And one of the questions was, "Who wrote Peter Pan?" to which she'd put Charles Barry . . . *and* spelt it with a Y at that. I mean, in all conscience I was obliged to give no marks for this. Charles Barry built the Houses of Parliament, I think. Anyway, he certainly didn't write Peter Pan. But when the answers were read out, and she heard the word Barry, and saw my big black X . . . oh, boy, she made a scene like a Beatles riot. She said, not only had I tried to drown her but now this: and if I didn't reverse my decision she'd take it right up to the Captain. So of course I had to, which was morally very painful. For the

95

rest of the voyage she was always catching me up and rubbing it in, and of course I couldn't get away at any speed because I'd got half my left foot in plaster.

I don't think there's time to go through the rest of this drawer. Not in any detail, anyway. I've got some United Nations book-matches, printed "Delegates' Dining Room". As souvenirs go, I suppose they're a bit marginal, but they do remind me of a day in New York, when I'd been to see over the U.N. building and then set off on my own to find the Empire State, and couldn't, even though I knew I was in the right street. I still don't know how this happened, because it's fourteen hundred and seventy feet high; and somehow you can't stop people in Fifth Avenue and ask them to point out a thing that size. So I never did find it.

Then I've got some bits of tesselated pavement from the Vatican, and they remind me that I shouldn't have been in Rome at all if the Italian Railways hadn't lost our luggage at Genoa and sent it there by mistake. I went over the Vatican while my wife was trying to get it back.

And lastly—well, I mean, all I've room for—there's the spare stopper for an inflatable beach-bed we bought in Spain, with an instructions leaflet wrapped round it in Spanish. This reminds me that I carried that confounded bed, fully inflated in a high wind, all the way from the shops and along half a mile of beach, because I thought the old Spanish lady who'd sold it to me had said that I mustn't deflate it because it was filled with dangerous gas. However, when my slightly Spanish-speaking wife read the instructions she explained that the old girl had simply been warning me not to clean it with Benzine.

Actually, I never really believed this interpretation. I still think it was an unexploded bed, and when we came home, I took care we forgot to pack it. You never know. Funny things can happen in foreign parts. And I've got the souvenirs to prove it.

ROYAL HOMES
THROUGH THE CENTURIES

Queen Elizabeth II has three official residences, Buckingham Palace, Windsor Castle, and Holyrood house, and two private houses, Sandringham and Balmoral. In the spring and at weekends she often stays at Windsor. In the late summer she resides at her Scottish home. Christmas is usually spent on her Norfolk estate. This seems to involve much travelling but by the standard of former kings and queens she is poorly served, for example, Elizabeth I regularly used fourteen palaces and was constantly journeying from one to the other. The saying that Queen Elizabeth slept here has some cause for credibility.

Most monarchs have had their favourite homes where they could indulge themselves more freely than in their palaces, dogged by court officials—great houses such as Hampton Court which Henry VIII received as a gift from Cardinal Wolsey and which became the honeymoon home for many royal couples; Audley End was Charles II's favourite house, and William and Mary's private country residence was Kensington Palace.

The following pages of photographs illustrate other royal homes which were the private delight of past kings and queens.

RICHMOND PALACE was a very ancient royal home. Edward III died at Shene, as it was known, in 1377, and so did Richard II's consort in 1394. The old manor fell into disrepair and was restored by Henry V, but in 1498 it was razed by a great fire. This gave Henry VII (left) the chance to rebuild it as a magnificent residence, surmounted by fourteen turrets.

Queen Mary spent much time at this riverside palace, and Queen Elizabeth found it suited her well, often held court there, and died at Richmond in 1603 at the age of seventy. It was rarely used again as a royal home and soon became a ruin. Little remains now except the restored buildings known as the Old Palace, and the Wardrobe and the old Gatehouse.

GREENWICH PALACE was first known as 'Bella Court' in the early 15th century and then as 'Placentia'. Henry VIII was born there and so were his daughters Princesses Mary and Elizabeth. It was his favourite home just as his father's was Richmond. Huge banquets and tournaments were held at Greenwich and the palace resounded to the boisterous life of Henry's court.

Queen Elizabeth often stayed there and so did James I, and it was the latter's wife, Anne of Denmark, who commissioned the architect Inigo Jones in the early 17th century to build a new house (Queen's House) there. It was completed for Charles I's wife Henrietta Maria. Charles II demolished the old palace and, in the reign of William and Mary, Christopher Wren built Greenwich Hospital which is now the Royal Naval College.

BUCKINGHAM PALACE is built on the site of several houses. First Goring House was erected in about 1640 where James I had his mulberry orchard to feed his silkworms. It was destroyed by fire in 1674 and was replaced by Arlington House, which in its turn was demolished and rebuilt by the Duke of Buckingham. This splendid house was acquired by George III in 1762 and here, it was said, the King and Queen Charlotte (left) live 'like turtle doves together, bring up their children, play music, interfere with no living soul'.

The illustration shows the drawing of Queen's House, as it was then known, by Pugin with figures by Thomas Rowlandson, as published in Ackermann's *Microcosm of London*, 1808.

In 1825 John Nash remodelled it as a palace and added two wings. A frontispiece, joining the wings, was built in Queen Victoria's reign and the front was re-faced by Sir Aston Webb in 1913.

BRIGHTON PAVILION is a monument to the Prince Regent (right) who first visited Brighton in 1783 and acquired the site in 1800. Shortly afterwards John Nash, the famous "Regency" architect, built the bizarre oriental residence which was quickly dubbed 'The Kremlin' and about which Sydney Smith commented that 'the dome of St. Paul's must have come down to Brighton and pupped'.

Here the future George IV entertained on a lavish scale and spent wild nights in the company of his lively but none too reputable friends. William IV and his Queen enjoyed staying at the Pavilion, but Queen Victoria and Prince Albert disliked the place for it was too frivolous for them. In 1850 it was bought by the Brighton Corporation and it is now fully restored.

KENSINGTON PALACE was bought by William and Mary in 1689. It was then known as Nottingham House and was situated at a convenient distance from Westminster but lay in a rural setting. Soon Sir Christopher Wren was commissioned to enlarge it with the fine buildings shown below.

Here, in a house they had made very much their own, both William and Mary died, and Queen Anne lived and died here also. George II frequently stayed at Kensington. Victoria was born there and, at the age of 18, learnt of her accession to the throne at six o'clock in the morning on June 20, 1837.

Now it continues to be a royal house, for the Duchess of Kent and her family have apartments at Kensington and part of it is also the home of Princess Margaret and her husband.

OSBORNE HOUSE on the Isle of Wight was acquired by Queen Victoria in 1845, five years after her marriage, and Prince Albert closely supervised its rebuilding in the Italianate style. Here the Queen and her family found the privacy they craved at 'our Island home', where they had their own beach and an extensive estate which the children explored under the direction of their father.

When Prince Albert died in 1861, Osborne House was retained, in the Queen's eyes, as a monument to her husband's memory. Here, dressed in mourning black, she spent much of the remaining forty years of her life and here she died.

King Edward VII, on his succession, gave Osborne to the nation and it became a convalescent home for officers, but the general public can now visit some rooms of the house which remain at they were in Queen Victoria's time.

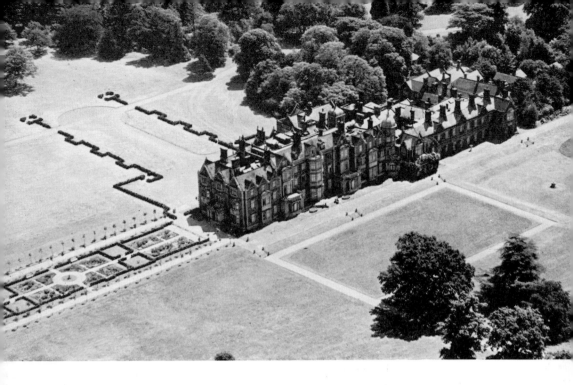

SANDRINGHAM HOUSE was almost entirely rebuilt after it was acquired for Queen Victoria's eldest son in 1861. Here the Prince and Princess of Wales entertained lavishly and the Prince was proud to be a squire and landlord.

Nearby lies York Cottage where George, Duke of York, and his bride Princess May spent their honeymoon. They retained it as their family house for 33 years. 'Dear old Sandringham', George V once said, 'the place I love better than anywhere in the world', and George VI was equally attached to the house and the estate for he was a country man at heart. Now Sandringham is a favourite home for the Queen and her family.

Reporting a Royal Wedding

by Anne Sharpley

REPORTING FOR AN evening paper is largely a matter of being able to run, write without thinking for too long, and fix up exits, telephones and cable communications. Reporters who work for morning papers have more time in which to write (unless the story breaks after midnight) and can afford to be less frantic in their requisitioning of phones and cable facilities. Yet it seems to me that they must miss the marvellous excitement of having to get it away at once. Their stories must often languish. It is the *immediacy* of reporting for an evening paper with editions going away all the time that I love. And I have discovered after fifteen years in newspapers—the last seven on the London *Evening Standard* —that the mind is a wonderful machine—if you only let it do the work for you.

So many times I have run to a phone or a cable office stricken with certainty I wouldn't be able to find a single word to describe what I had just seen, heard, or found out. But under the pressure of necessity out the words have poured, in a dutiful, properly-ordered stream without so much as a glance at the notebook I had been so busily filling.

Princess Margaret's wedding for instance. I dictated nearly two thousand words in just under an hour, which works out at just under a word every two seconds. Preparing sentences beforehand is no good—they have a way of seeming lifeless within the much more vivid material that the actuality has produced. You have somehow to give not merely the picture of what you have just seen—the camera can do that much better in any case—but the experience. The smell, the sense of being there, even if it is highly-personalized—you must communicate that emotion.

Of course you go through a certain amount of preliminary swotting up first. But this is more often to fulfil an anxious need to do something about a big event before it happens. So you learn the curious names of the remotest official at a royal function, re-read the Abbey history, try to sort out, once again, the European relations of the royal family (supposing one of them fainted and you didn't know which it was—there's no chance to scramble across to where they lie fainting to inquire). Happily, in the end, your homework is usually discarded. But it gives the mind a sort of breakfast to start the great day on.

The day before the wedding I had gone to Westminster Abbey, located my seat, and found that from the point of view of reporting in an intimate style, it was not very helpful. I had binoculars but although the press positions were fairly concealed I envisaged being told to "put those things away" by the vergers who are not open to the argument that the camera-men use telescopic lenses, so why shouldn't the reporter. In a binocular shop I found what might be the answer, a pair of spectacles with fixed binocular attachments, not very strong, but able to bring me two or three times nearer the centre of things. I was glad of this later as through them I observed one of those small but significant moments in what would otherwise be rather routine magnificence.

Mr. Armstrong-Jones as he was waiting for the Princess to arrive was, quite naturally, restlessly interlacing his fingers. Suddenly I noticed him grin and look down at his hands. I, through my spectacle-binoculars, looked down too. He was playing the old game of "There's the church and there's the steeple. Open the doors and see all the people". He was just about to open the doors and see all the people when the Queen's procession arrived and he had to stand up and nod gravely to the members of the great family into which he was marrying. Perhaps it seems a trivial point—but to me it illustrated how his delightful and impish sense of humour had not deserted him even in that solemn moment.

Since the spectacle-binoculars were set for a distance they were of course no use for looking down at my notebook—or for writing notes.

But through such exigencies as interviewing people in the dark and writing under tables during banquets, I can scribble happily and illegibly away, either in shorthand or longhand, under the firm delusion that what I am writing will be useful later.

Looking through those notes now, I realize that I did in fact put some of the phrases I scribbled down into my notes into the newspaper story, such points as the dust on the canopies of the tombs at the side of the sacrarium, and such phrases as "trumpets, sound both exquisite and violent", "Archbish'—shines like sugar-loaf", all of which got into the story, although in fact there was no time to look them up in the notebook as I dictated it. The wedding over, there came a fine test of journalistic ethics. The wedding guests in the North transept had decided with good-mannered accord to let Sir Winston Churchill lead the way from the Abbey by the North door. He would, I estimated, take four, possibly five, minutes to walk from the Abbey and traverse the path to the gate opposite the House of Commons, St. Stephen's Porch.

Could I afford to wait, respectfully, with the rest? I had already made certain by timely moves, that I was going to be the first to leave the press gallery. I decided I would run for it. If I ran quickly enough I would be actually off the other end of the path before Sir Winston put foot on it. I hope it was respect for the great man that gave me an extra turn of speed as I raced for St. Stephen's Porch. Through the empty Westminster Hall, echoing to my impertinent heels, I ran, and then up the stairs to the House of Commons press gallery. I had anticipated all sorts of difficulties in getting into the Commons, and so had arranged for phones to be held for me at three different points near the Abbey. (At the Grace Kelly wedding where I had not made such flexible arrangements I had physically to hack my way through the police cordon, vigorously assisted by a sports-loving, police-hating French crowd.)

After nearly an hour in a House of Commons phonebox (which was every bit as cramped, Gothic, and airless as one would expect) I fell out exhausted, the story and the tension over, and not a very clear idea, as usual, what I had just dictated. I was hot and tired—and the parquet floor of the press gallery looked invitingly cool. There was no one about—so I thought I would lie down for just a minute. So crossing my ankles and my wrists in what I thought was a proper medieval fashion suitable to the place and occasion, and putting my hat on my chest, I lay there and relaxed.

It was then that the gentleman from *The Times* came into the gallery. He looked at me and realized either I was ill, drunk, dead—or I wasn't there. He decided I wasn't there. Stepping quickly and neatly past he left me to the cool floor and the struggle to remember just what it was I had said in those two thousand words over the phone.

Unusual Offices

by Philip Holland

PEOPLE WHO ADVERTISE holiday accommodation to let aren't usually coy about the attractions of the property they have to offer. On the contrary, in fact—as some of us know to our cost. But in Ireland, it seems, there are some at least who are careful not to overdo it. Take this advertisement from the personal column of *The Times* for example:

"Available owing to last minute cancellation, unusual furnished House on sea front, south-west Ireland; four bedrooms with hot and cold, etc., in each; everything supplied. Vacant 1st July (near Bantry)."

Unusual? Now what on earth do they mean by that? Architecturally unusual, perhaps. What about these etceteras in the bedrooms? I mean, apart from the furniture, it seems to me that there's not much you can have in a bedroom, once you've got the h. and c. fixed up. Of course one does hear of these extraordinary bedrooms that very rich people have, with cupids in the ceiling and polar-bear skins on the floor, and a television set which disappears into the wall when you want to go to sleep. But surely, if this were the answer, they'd say so, and not just lump all these expensive luxuries together as "etc.". I don't think this can be the answer. Bantry Bay is a charming place, but cupids and bearskins don't seem to fit in, somehow.

"Unusual". Well if it isn't the etceteras, what is it? I see that the house is described as being "on the sea front". Now is this, perhaps, an understatement? Is the house not so much *on* the seafront as *in* it? I mean there are a lot of rocks in that part of the world, and a house built on a rock out in the bay, cut off by the sea, except for an hour or so at low water, from the high life of Bantry, could I suppose be fairly described as "unusual". Certainly you couldn't complain about being too far from the sea, not when it's liable to break into your bedroom and flood your etceteras.

I think we may be on the right track here, because I see the advertisement also says "everything supplied". Of course it's perfectly true that if you're out there, perched on this storm-lashed, sea-swept rock, you would be very glad indeed to see, through your telescope, the dot on the horizon which meant that a boat was on its way with your supplies for the week, and you'd need to be pretty sure that everything was supplied before the boat shoved off again. No popping round the corner to the shop when you find you've run out of etceteras.

But perhaps the best clue of all to just what is "unusual" about this house is the reason given for its availability. "Available", the advertisement says, "owing to last minute cancellation". How "last minute" I wonder? I have a strong feeling that a family actually spent the first night of their holiday in this unusual house, and that one night was enough. And why? Well, they were prepared to have etceteras in the bedrooms, and to be marooned on a rock, and to be supplied with everything, weather permitting, but what they didn't know, until that first night, what finally tipped the scales, was that they weren't the only people in the house. The little folk were there—the Leprechauns—and when the little folk take over, then a house does become very unusual indeed. Things disappear. Things go bump in the night. Aunt Tabitha, who came on the holiday with you, vanishes, and re-appears two days later on the sea shore, with a far-away look in her eyes and wild-flowers in her hair.

Yes, very unusual. One last thing. The paper in which the advertisement appeared was dated the 13th, and the house, said the advertisement, was available from the first. So at least you can be sure that it's in Ireland.

Black Mountain Fiord

by Leslie Gardiner

THE CAPTAIN'S VOICE came over the ship's radio, recommending everyone to be on deck first thing in the morning for a sight of the prettiest port in Europe. We were coasting down the mountainous seaboard of Yugoslavia, in and out among the wild green islands with the unpronounceable names; the scent of rosemary and of lemons and oranges came off the land. Tomorrow it would be Kotor, southward in Montenegro.

At 6 a.m. on the dot, the ship turned in towards the land, a gap appeared in that mountainous curtain of coastline and we squeezed through, as though entering a smuggler's cove. I almost believed one of the officers when he told me the inhabitants used to put a chain across and lock the place up at night. When I saw the great iron rings rusting on the headlands and consulted the chart and saw that it was actually called Channel of the Chain, I knew he was *not* pulling my leg.

About a hundred yards separated those headlands, where we passed through. But beyond lay a fiord, the only fiord in southern Europe. And from one headland to the other by land, around the multifarious inlets, would have been all of fifty miles. The ship twisted and turned and wriggled its way inland, often faced with solid barriers of cliff that made it certain she must turn sharp round or run ashore. But every time she found another gap. The deep blue of the Adriatic shaded to deep green, jellyfish like outsize bath sponges drifted by and the thump of our engines reverberated off the mountainside. Even a small cargo vessel like ours had her work cut out, to make some of those tight turns. As my fellow-passenger said, it would be a grand sight—and a heart-in-mouth one too—to see the *Andes* or another of the big cruising liners come through. They do sometimes.

The mountains grew higher and steeper and clustered round more closely, as though to prevent the sea penetrating any further. We side-stepped for the last time and emerged on a big lake. To the south the cliffs rose grey and bare, laid waste by the sun. On the north they were green and shady, and sprinkled with orchards. A miniature Byzantine church, pure white with its characteristic blue dome, squatted in mid-channel—afloat, one would have thought; there was no island visible, no means of support except its own perfect reflection. Further on we passed a clump of cypresses, a ruined castle and a row of fruit bushes, all distributed in the same fashion on the smooth, tideless surface. A rise of six inches in the water level would have inundated them all; so would the ship's wash, if we had not been going dead slow.

Twenty miles from the open sea, at the end of the lake, on the only patch of level ground for miles around, and that not much bigger than a cricket pitch, we saw Kotor. Four thousand feet up, bleak and windswept, the black hills of Montenegro stood guard on the delicate scene. (Montenegro, of course, means Black Mountain.) As soon as we got ashore we made for those peaks because the view, over the ramifications of the fiord we had just traversed, is one of the great experiences of Balkan travel.

So, for that matter, is the road up and down, with more hairpin bends to the yard than any I know. On the descent we were poised several times for a high dive into the brilliant green waters of the fiord, and the last lap, after we had sampled the wild figs and pomegranates at the roadside, positively dropped us out of the sky, on to the red pantiled roofs of Kotor. This jumble of wynds and alleyways and catacombs and medieval history huddles inside a thick Venetian wall and, as though that were not enough, is protected by the ruin of a once-powerful Venetian fortress. One invader that never got into Kotor was the motor vehicle. The little town is exclusive to pedestrians, and even they have a problem getting through the main gate if they happen to be on the plump side.

I wanted to try a zig-zag precipice walk to the fortress, and to explore the limestone gorges of a torrent that came leaping off the Black Mountains. But the ship's siren was echoing round the fiord. We departed. I sat on the after-deck and for the next couple of hours watched the incredible panorama of our inland voyage unroll again, this time in reverse.

When we squeezed out of the Channel of the Chain and came into open sea and the entrance to Kotor fiord closed up like the entrance to Ali Baba's cave . . . I wondered then whether the prettiest harbour in Europe really existed, behind that blank wall of coastline, or whether I had been dozing in my deck-chair and imagined it all.

Crosswords

by Alan Melville

YOU WOULD THINK, wouldn't you, that the main function of crossword puzzles (and I am an addict) would be to instruct, amuse, occasionally irritate, but never really to bring out the nasty mean streaks in human nature. I'm not so sure.

My mother, from whom I suppose I inherited the addiction, used to do the crossword in the *Scotsman* every morning while she was having her elevenses. She had a slap-happy, carefree approach to the clues which was rather endearing and in a way typical of my mother: if 16 across was an eight-letter word beginning with T and the clue was "Famous Verdi Opera", and she wrote in "Trovatore" and found to her horror that that had nine letters, she just put the final "e" in the margin. Well, there was no harm done: with any luck she might still get the word going down starting with the V, just as she'd have done if she'd put in "Traviata" in the first place. By the time she'd finished the puzzle, I must admit that the margins round it looked a bit messy—like a handkerchief that's had its hem ripped off by the laundry—but at least the only person she was fooling was herself: and I suppose the compiler of the puzzle.

I find, however, that crosswords bring out some very undesirable traits in people's characters: in mine, certainly. This is particularly true when I'm doing a crossword in the train, and someone else in the compartment is doing the same crossword. I have the technique pretty well worked out now on the early-morning (or fairly early-morning) train up to London, when you can usually rely on at least a couple of other commuters getting out their ball-points and having a go at the puzzle in that paper once billed as the one Top People read.

If I finish the puzzle first—and it has happened at least twice in '64 and once in '65—there is infinite satisfaction in giving a little sigh, half of triumph and half of regret, that the thing turned out to be so childishly simple that morning, putting your ball-point back in the inside pocket and nonchalantly throwing the paper across on to the vacant seat next to the moron who's still struggling with the quotation from *As You Like It* in the bottom left-hand corner. I say nonchalantly, but you have to be jolly careful in throwing the paper across the compartment: naturally it must land puzzle-side up, to let the chap see that you really have finished it, but it must also land at an angle which makes it difficult if not down-right impossible for him to see what you've put in the bottom left-hand corner without craning his neck and giving it away that he's cribbing.

I have been known, just for the hell of it, to ignore the news of the day and concentrate on the puzzle over breakfast: not filling it in, but waiting until I get on the train and then seeming to solve the clues at break-neck speed to the mortification of the man sitting opposite. In fact, I'll be perfectly frank, because I feel we know each other well enough by now: once, I finished and filled in the whole of the puzzle before catching the 8.36 from Brighton. And I was so enamoured of myself because of this remarkable feat—this is what I mean, it brings out the worst in you—that I bought another copy of the paper and appeared to have rattled off the entire problem piece by the time the train got to Preston Park, which is the first station out of Brighton. I threw it across to the vacant seat pretty nonchalantly that morning, I can tell you. I spent the rest of the journey looking out of the window and humming, as though wishing there was something else to do to fill in the time; by East Croydon the man opposite was livid.

I have a friend in the country who does the same puzzle as I do every day, and occasionally—very occasionally—if I'm stuck I so demean myself as to ring her up in the evening and, after inquiring about the children's health and the state of her asparagus bed, I say, "By the way, did you get

22 down?" "Well, of course," she says. " 'Agamemnon'. He was the husband of Clytemnestra. I thought everyone knew that. As a matter of fact, I thought it was one of the easiest puzzles for months. I finished it before I did the bedrooms." She cheats, of course. She pretends that she never uses dictionaries or books of reference. I've seen them lying all over the place—and at seven o'clock in the evening when she's in a panic to get the puzzle finished before I drop in for supper. She lies, too. All crossword addicts do. If you're frank and honest, as I am in these matters, and say "Look, I'm baffled. What in Heaven's name is 27 across—'next Scottish Tory Prime Minister question mark'?" she says, "I can't remember. I know I got it, because it was something quite obvious, but the paper's upstairs." Then she rings back the next morning and says "I've just remembered—it was Macheath, of course," but by then she's seen yesterday's solution and has all the reference books out for today's puzzle.

It's extraordinary that people who are normally honest, straightforward, God-fearing, responsible citizens should be so deceitful over a silly little thing like a crossword puzzle. I can't wait for the next time I manage to finish mine at breakfast and buy another copy of the paper for the benefit of that man sitting opposite me on the 8.36.

FARAWAY PLACES

On the Veranda

by Rosamund Harcourt-Smith

SOME YEARS BEFORE we learnt that Imperialism was a dirty word, my family lived for a time in India. The official house allotted to my father had been built in the seventeenth century at the time of Shah Jehan when Italian styles were all the rage; colonnaded verandas supporting Palladian pediments ran on every side of the house; in rainy weather water spouted from the beaks of bronze cranes jutting from the roof.

The west veranda was wide and long as a ballroom, carpeted and furnished with sofas and chairs. Beneath the columns stood pots of red salvia, blue hortensia and white daisies. This patriotic scheme had been the custom of the house since Queen Victoria's Diamond Jubilee. Above the flowers a host of humming birds, no bigger than a thumb-nail, whirled their sequined wings as they thrust needle-beaks into the honey.

Every evening when the sun was low, a cool scent rose from the gardens as a crew of urchins, armed with cans, watered the lawns. The children were naked save for loin-cloths and puggarees. Although they kept their bright eyes modestly lowered, they seemed always to be convulsed with laughter the moment they saw me. Sometimes their mirth resulted in horse-play and a puggaree would get knocked off. Then with squeals of outraged modesty, for all the world like English children who had lost their knickers, the brats dived behind a bed of canna lilies to rewind the offending rag round a shaved pate. It was improper to appear bare-headed in public and the head gardener was a great stickler for etiquette.

When word got round that the Small Miss Sahib was amused by the antics of the garden-boys, every father in the compound was set on showing me his offspring. When I went on to my own veranda in the early morning some child of ten would be sure to scuttle up with a tiny baby balanced on her hip. I never failed to admire the pretty cherubs, slip into the tiny hand a coin or tie a string of beads round the touching, tender neck.

At the far end of the great west veranda two elderly tailors stitched away from nine to four. By reason of the gowns they wore they were known as the Green Durzi and the Blue Durzi. They loathed each other.

Green Durzi was a beautiful old man with a calm, benevolent expression. He was not particularly adept at his trade, indeed, most of the time he was employed in making uniforms for the house-servants which, since they had been in fashion since the days of Warren Hastings, he could hardly go wrong with.

Blue Durzi was quite another plate of curry. You had only to show him a picture in a fashion magazine and he had puzzled out the pattern in no time. He was a tiny slip of a man, his cross, whiskered face reminded one of the marmoset while his blue robe seemed to conceal no more than a slip of bamboo.

My mother worried about the frail old man's health. To help fatten him he was given a pint of milk daily and it gratified my mother to notice that every evening when he stumped off down the drive he did, in fact, look fatter. What she did not understand was that his bulk consisted of odds and ends of material left over from his cutting-out, rolled up and stuffed under the blue gown.

Once he lost his head completely and made off with six yards of silk intended for my mother's night-gowns. Unfortunately for him he had not secured the stuff and when he went to the pantry for his milk, a train of pink fell from under the blue gown. The head-servant, Gulam, spotted it.

"You stupid old robber," Gulam said, "the Lady-Sahib may be soft with you, but don't imagine she'll stand for wholesale robbery!"

Apart from the scraps of material, Blue Durzi had two great interests in life, one was to steal as many reels of white sewing-cotton as he could, the other to get my mother to buy a new sewing-machine when the old one would become his by use and wont. None of the bazaar shops sold good quality cotton, the most they could provide were little balls of inferior thread used for tacking. Number fifty Best White Machine cotton arrived in boxes of a dozen from Calcutta. It was Blue Durzi's self-appointed task to acquire as many spools as possible before the box emptied, to this end he devised an admirable plan.

He saved the empty reels, took them home and employed his sharp little nephew to wind on the inferior cotton, which he used on our sewing machine while the new reels he was able to peddle in the bazaar. He had a large and ready market; sometimes his clients' demands made the old boy's greed outrun his discretion. There was one dramatic occasion when he demanded fresh cotton three days running.

"Weiss cot-ton?" he would ask my mother, scratching the carpet coyly with a bare foot.

"*More* white cotton? But Durzi, you've had two in the last two days, you can't have used a hundred yards yet? You must have mislaid the reel, go and look for it."

"No weiss cot-ton," said the ancient crossly and stamped off. A couple of hours later my sister found him, still cross-legged, head sunk on breast, apparently unconscious. Should a doctor be called for? Gulam was sent to inquire; he came back giggling. "Durzi saying not ill, cannot work, no weiss cot-ton!"

After this episode Blue Durzi failed to come to work for three weeks, and he let it be known that he intended to find another job where his employers were less stingy. However, one day he turned up in his usual place and no more was said.

The demands for white cotton became less intense, but he redoubled his attack on the sewing-machine.

"Sewing machine very bad, not work well, broke. Lady Sahib buying new kind?" he asked repeatedly. By the end of two months she was brainwashed, a new machine was sent from Calcutta and the old one passed on to Durzi.

Some weeks later, while I was poking about in the bazaar, searching for coral necklaces, old embroidery, silver beads, Blue Durzi's nephew accosted me, smiling and salaaming, he was now sixteen. He had gone into the tailoring business and had his own establishment—if you can call a hole in the wall roofed over with kerosene tins an establishment. I was shown the tiny shop. On the table stood our old sewing-machine.

"Very nice machine, very good kind, English make," said the boy proudly, caressing the handle.

"Magnificent," I agreed. "Where did you get it?"

"Uncle buy cheap, sell me, I pay back moneys."

"Your uncle is very clever," I said.

The boy beamed. "Very clever man, very number one Durzi."

Sometimes I wondered if saintly Green Durzi never felt qualms of envy, realizing as he must surely have done, Blue's accomplished trickery, yet he seemed happy enough. One day however, he revolted against Blue's bad manners, his jeers and spite, yet found a way to avoid him without losing face.

A pair of doves had built their nest in a cornice above the place where the tailors sat. All day long their cooing echoed across the veranda. In India doves are not regarded as emblems of peace or fidelity, instead they are noted for their licentious behaviour. This gave Green Durzi an idea. He came to my mother and asked if he could move his seat to the south veranda.

"The south? But Durzi, it's so hot there, surely you will be very uncomfortable?"

"Better to suffer on earth than to burn in hell," was the unexpected answer. He explained that the doves were the trouble. Doubtless God had created them as a warning against lechery, but how could such a one as he, a respected man and a grandfather many times over, sit all day listening to their improper conversation, it was not to be supported. Thereafter he sat in stifling solitude uncontaminated by the dove's coarse words and freed from the jeers and jibes of his colleague.

One of the most interesting servants was Moti Lal. He had started life as a farm-hand in Orissa. His skin was so intensely dark it seemed blue, the colour of Ganesh, the elephant god. He suffered from permanent catarrh.

He was a door-keeper, a Government servant, dressed in scarlet and gold, fine enough to the eye, but kept to the uninspiring task of carrying letters or acting as night-porter. However, he had his ambitions; he itched to become a house-servant.

In those days "service" meant something more than having your wind-screen wiped in a garage. As the servant in a big house, you were trusted by your employers, looked up to by your equals and, above all, you became part of a family life which in turn you adopted as your own. Moti Lal's chance came two days before I was due to go to Delhi for a round of Christmas parties. My personal bearer fell ill. Who was to accompany me, who was to iron my dresses, make my bed, dust my room and generally make himself useful to my hostess? My mother decided I could not burden my hosts by arriving without a servant, and Gulam, as always, came to my aid.

"Moti Lal," he told my mother, "very good man, very nice, clean, taking Miss Sahib to Delhi, looking after well."

"Moti Lal?" said my mother. "But he's never been a house-servant, how could he know what to do?"

"Moti Lal learning, iron clothes very well, wash, look after. Very nice man, Lady Sahib soon seeing."

For the next two days Moti Lal stood, snuffling and patient between the ice-box and the hot-case in the vast pantry. From time to time Gulam darted in to give him further briefing on his duties.

Leaving for Delhi was always an adventure. The train drew into Patna station before dawn. The platform was crowded with untidy human bundles, poor travellers dozing as they waited to be carried off up-country.

You had to pick your way carefully to avoid knocking over a cooking-pot or treading on some outstretched hand twitching in uneasy sleep. The cold, sour smell of sleeping humanity was nevertheless, to me, the first step towards the road to romance, freedom, fun—to pale blue facings on uniforms of the Viceroy's staff, to the shimmer of rajah's jewels, to the loan of chestnut-shining polo ponies, to admiration, kisses, and above all, to change.

Moti Lal had been warned that at every station along the line he must come to the door of my carriage and ask if I wanted anything. On no account—and here Gulam was at pains to warn the guard as well—must any male person of any kind be allowed inside my compartment. Moti Lal acquitted himself magnificently. He might have been a lady's maid of years' standing, discreet, painstaking, spotlessly clean. His great triumph came when my hostess asked if he would help serve at a dinner-party she was giving to the Viceroy. Moti Lal was dotty with excitement. No footman trained in the rigid decorum of a great English country house could have behaved better. He well knew he would be one up on the staff at home when he returned; he had served the Viceroy his very self. Hand to the left, remove from the right, pick up the fallen napkins, fill glasses, don't scuttle. How Moti Lal learnt it all I can't imagine. Old Bhudoo, our head table servant, was far too jealous a character to have passed on his learning to an iron-dark peasant boy.

I was devoted to Bhudoo. His calm face breathed the deceptive saintliness of a two-year-old child. His great speciality was a chocolate cake which had the consistency of sugary sand, was as light as a feather and heavily frosted. Once he left in a huff after a row with some other servant. He was never coming back, he let it be known. As usual Gulam stepped in; after a series of incompetent stopgaps, he came to my mother saying, "Bhudoo a very sad man thinking how Lady Sahib missing her nice cakes, no one to make sweets for the Miss Sahibs. Bhudoo only a baby-man, more better Lady Sahib having him back?"

In a day or so back he came, fat and beaming in his starched white robe, presenting his famous cake, waiting as always until we cut it and exclaimed at its excellence: "How delicious, Bhudoo, the very best you've ever made!"

Then he sidled off to the pantry like a conjuror who has brought off an almost impossible trick.

Every afternoon when the weather was neither too hot nor too cold, tea was laid on the veranda. Nearly always there were a few guests. One visitor was an elderly Maharajah with a white beard and a high, squeaky voice. He was so tiny that when he sat in one of the broad, overstuffed chairs, his legs stuck straight out in front of him like a child's. He was always dressed to kill and his magnificent clothes and jewellery were the usual starting point of our conversations. "What a splendid ornament you're wearing in your puggaree, Highness. Surely that cannot be glass. Is it crystal?" "Nay, nay, Miss Sahib, it is a diamond." "A diamond—but such a huge stone and cut like a slice of cake. Has it been in your family long?" "Ninety years, Miss Sahib, my grandfather won it in a wager from the Nisal." "A wager—what was the wager?" The old man giggled delightedly. "Nay, nay, Miss Sahib, I must not tell. It was young men's jokes, not for the ears of young ladies." Then, lest the young men's jokes be altogether missed, he added, "My grandfather was a very powerful man, very strong." My mother looked down her nose. She didn't care for young men's jokes, even ninety-year-old ones.

Another friend of whom we were very fond lived in a huge Gothic fort on a bend of the Ganges. In rainy weather water lapped against the ancient foundations with the sound of the sea. It was a romantic place, the walls six feet deep. We were devoted to this man and he in turn loved us and found nothing to complain of in the Raj. One thing puzzled him. My father's position surely provided endless opportunities for "Scris". What passed his understanding was why such chances were neglected. Why, for instance, had my mother covered the innumerable chairs and sofas of our house in a sort of fine burlap made locally? The cream cotton piped with red was pretty enough, but hardly fitting for such an elegant house.

"Your visit to Benares—how did that go off?" asked my mother one day. "Thank you, thank you, Lady Sahib." Our friend raised his hands, palms joined, in that charming Eastern gesture of respect and thanks. "God was good to me. I bought many yards of fine King cob to cover my chairs and sofas." He paused for a moment, fingering the arm of the chair he sat on. "Why does not the Lady Sahib buy such stuff for these chairs?" "King cob," laughed my mother, "is the very grandest old brocade, but that's far too expensive for me. These covers do very well and they wash like dusters." "Mm, not good dusters," murmured our friend disapprovingly.

Once I begged him to bring his little grandson to see us. The baby toddled in holding his grandfather's finger. He wore tiny white trousers, a beautiful brocade coat and a pink puggaree on his head. He sat on a foot stool with all the grace and dignity of an infant Louis XV. Presently I noticed him sucking what I took to be a huge green sweet tied to a gold cord, to save him from swallowing it I supposed. "Will he not get his beautiful coat sticky with so large a sweet?" I asked. "Not a sweetie, not a sweetie. It is my big emerald; he is cutting his teeth," was the reply.

Sometimes we were invited back to the riverside palace. The huge rooms were horribly furnished with late Victorian stuff which seemed to bear no relation to any furniture made before or since. That the chairs were covered with magnificent brocade seemed only to accentuate the essential poverty of their design. While we sat talking, trays were handed round loaded with Indian sweetmeats, surely the most delicious in the world. After a while conversation would flag and the moment I longed for arrive. A maid would announce that the ladies were waiting for me and I'd be carried off to the women's quarters. There a host of pretty girls, nieces, daughters-in-law, grand-daughters, stripped off my dress, my shoes and stockings, wound me in some exquisite sari, clasped a precious necklace, hung earrings from my pierced ears. I always regretted my nose was not pierced. A diamond nose ring can be very alluring. When I was rigged out I was taken back into the drawing room to be admired. There

I would draw the sari in mock modesty across my face, as the girls told the old man they had a young virgin for his pleasure, and squealed with delight at my play acting.

Luckily my mother had never mastered the language or her strong sense of decorum would have been outraged. The following day, trays of mangoes, lichees, peaches and more of those delicious sweets would arrive at our house. This is a graceful Indian custom whereby the residue of food from the party is sent to the house of the chief guest for the regalement of her servants. Gulam, our head servant, always managed to fill a dish with fabulous delicacies scented with rose, amber, pistachio and flecked with real gold leaf. "Lady Sahib liking very much," he would say, setting the dish before my mother. "More pity letting servants eat all up."

Not all our guests were so well disposed towards the Raj. Young Mrs. Boase had been educated at Girton. She disapproved of the entire English set-up. Her large, round face was that of a woman of twenty-five. Her huge bulk suggested an indulgent fifty. Little Mr. Boase was a son of a millionaire steel manufacturer. Unlike most young men of his age and class he never attended any of the Government universities and spoke with a sing-song lilt of an Eurasian using the slang of a Calcutta clerk. His wife's accent was, of course, impeccable. Mrs. Boase's notion of agreeable party conversation was to start a violent anti-British argument. "I do hope you had an opportunity when in Delhi to speak to the Viceroy about this matter of unemployment," she would say to my father. "It's a scandal that you English do nothing about it." Little Mr. Boase tried to stem his wife's flow, "No, no," he would cry, "you must not listen to my wife. She is a holy terror. She was educated at your Oxford college where ladies are taught to dispute. I tell her that since she come this side, she try to wear the pants in my house."

Mrs. Boase smiled affectionately at him, she treated him as if he were a child. "My husband's old-fashioned. He thinks women should only talk of clothes." "Well clothes are always fascinating," said my mother tactfully, "particularly when one can wear such lovely things as your sari."

But Mrs. Boase was not to be palmed off with tact. "But do you know how much the poor creatures in the factories are paid a day?" she would burst out. Mr. Boase began to giggle triumphantly. "I am telling my wife that not approving she should not buy," and this time Mrs. Boase was less indulgent with him. "That's not the point. If I don't buy others will. It's not the individual purchase, it's the entire system that's rotten." She glared at my father as if accusing him of all India's crime since the days of Akbar. Mr. Boase buzzed on like a happy little bee. "All the ladies of my house are stuck on politics. My young sister will go to meetings of Pandit Nehru." "I don't blame her," I murmured. "Of all the charmers, I long to meet him!" "That girl is a caution," went on Mr. Boase. "When the Pandit asked for funds for the Party, she threw her jewels on the stage. Her father had to ask for them back. All the young girls threw their jewels." "And did all the fathers ask for them back?" asked my father mildly. Mr. Boase rocked with laughter. His wife tapped the floor crossly with a foot bulging on either side of black patent leather straps. Caught up in her husband's mirth, we laughed too. "In our newly awakened state," Mrs. Boase went on earnestly, "it is inevitable that the politically conscious youth of India should allow emotion to over-ride prudence. Mune cannot be blamed for throwing her jewels." This fell flat. Boase was still mopping tears from his eyes, convulsed by my father's little joke, not that his wife blamed him. It was the fault of us frivolous English never taking anything seriously—how we maddened her.

When we left India for good, the Boases were among the many Indian friends who crowded the station to bid us farewell. With our shoulders entwined with garlands, fantastic creations of gold ribbon, jasmine or the humble marigold, we leaned from the carriage windows clasping one pair of boneless fluid hands, then another. Oriental emotions easily spill over, everyone wept. Then as our train drew out I saw Mrs. Boase snatch a handkerchief from her husband's pocket to mop the tears that furrowed her powdered cheeks. I felt sad for her. She might continue to cherish her pickled rod, but now that her English friends were leaving whom would she find to beat?

The Masterpiece

by Donald Brook

IN A JU-JU shrine in a village to the north of the Benue river there is, or was, a bottle of beer. In 1957 the crown cap was still intact and European civilization had not yet granted local insight into the nature of the contents or the means of extraction. It was an object of pure reverence, outshining its companion woodcarvings with a seductive symmetry and sheen, much as a Martian hat-rack might steal the limelight in the Tate Gallery—and perhaps does. Five or ten or twenty years before we came, a touring District Officer, obscurely disenchanted with his civilizing mission, had presented it to the village and maybe watched the ritual of its installation at the shrine. He must have left a happier man, that is if he left at all . . . there were bones. . . .

But our concern in Nigeria was with sculpture. The indigenous tradition is dying. White ants draw no clear moral distinction between art and furniture in their appetite for timber, and the museums must rescue what they can from the bush while there is still time. We were courteously shown the beer bottle, instructed that it was Not For Sale, and given a piece of priceless information.

A great carver, perhaps the greatest carver in the world we were told, lived a short way to the west. Communication between the villagers and ourselves was tenuous, consisting of the dozen words of Hausa spoken by the pagan headman, who had travelled in his youth, and the dozen words of Hausa spoken by John. To the ear of the outsider they didn't appear to be quite the corresponding dozen. But the "short way" to where the carver lived was confirmed in mime, and the name of the village clear enough. It was even marked on the printed action-painting (you might call it) which the Ordnance Survey whimsically describes as a map. Imagine a track cut through dripping and alien vegetables, rising and falling over boulders strewn by a careless and preoccupied giant and overlaid by a foot or more of rich red mud. Add a tropical downpour incredibly like the ones in the cinema, created by "special effects", a fallen tree or two, and the odd notice entreating you to "GIVE WAY . . . ELEPHANTS CROSSING". Natural hazards are endless, though a combination of two or more at a time can be, in a sense, final.

For the three in our party the end came smoothly and elegantly. With a gentle slow movement, like a dancer, our car rolled over on to its back and lowered us into several unlikely postures amongst the slow fall of camp-beds, biscuits and wooden statuary. Overhead the wheels rumbled in the air and the rain drummed on the floor. We lay for some time, caught in the almost voluptuary slow-motion dream of it all, until suddenly I heard a trickling sound, and a smell ominous of potential fire brought me to life.

"PETROL!" I shouted, heaved open a door, and laid violent hands on Margaret, intending to throw her as far away into the mud as my memory of screen heroics prompted. Her leg was hooked round a crate of tinned beef, and my push brought her head sharply against the side of the door. She fixed me with a look of implacable hatred and spoke with the devastating calm of one outraged beyond anger.

"Petrol," she said, "is only a few shillings a gallon. Let us be extravagant for once."

There was no fire.

We got out after a while. The wheels stopped, the rain stopped, and we were joined by two small naked boys with huge dark eyes and pro-tuberant bellies. One of them plucked at the mournful prongs of a tiny "bush piano", and the other swung a head of sticky palm-nuts slowly from side to side, like a censer. We all regarded the capsized car, prone in the mud, and spoke no word while the thin sad notes plinked on and young palm-nut picked a meditative nose with his free hand.

We walked. Nothing sustains human kind like a quest, a sense of expectation and hope. Ahead of us was one of the last great carvers working in a tradition that the world has condemned to death. When the fertilizers come in the fertility idols go out, and no one can balance the account with certainty. Here was to be found something pure and perfect and essentially unrepeatable; in a few years there will be no man alive who can make sculpture innocently and beautifully, uninfluenced by the clamour and unease brought by the knowledge of four thousand years of European fashions; sculpture with a place and purpose in society, woven into the fabric of belief and action . . . the mature fruit of a complete, unmechanized, civilization. This was our goal.

We walked through the mud, not talking much, each preoccupied with the thoughts of the village ahead, of woodcarving, and of the rise and fall of cities and cultures. We walked for miles, steaming.

After the ritual of greeting, the palaver and exchange of trivial gifts, the unconfessed embarrassments (who is going to carry twenty-one eggs of dubious age all that way back?) we were finally seated in an open enclosure within a rough circle of mud huts. The carver was a dignified old man, sparsely bearded, lean and wrinkled. He had the air of a sage or saint; an impression of importance without arrogance. He explained in Hausa that he would go and bring his best piece to show us. We waited impatiently. His best piece must be something considerable.

It was, and he came back wearing it.

Hewn from the trunk of a vast tree, and wrought to a finish of the utmost perfection, was a pair of wooden, European-type, circa eighteen-ninety, trousers. Every detail was lovingly and immaculately carved; buttonholes, seams, flies, belt-loops, pockets—everything. And the effort of supporting the considerable weight, combined with the rather curious walk to which he was necessarily constrained, left him no dignity whatever.

I don't know now why we didn't buy it, or them.

A Kafir's Revenge

by Michael Selzer

THE MESS SUBARDAR or sergeant greeted me with tears in his eyes: and then, to my surprise and embarrassment, threw his arms around me. "Sahib zinda hai, Sahib zinda hai,"—"The Sahib is alive"—he muttered over and over again.

"And why," I asked when I had managed to disengage myself, "should the Sahib not be alive?"

I had just returned to Chitral from a brief visit to the small nation known popularly as the Kafirs (their proper name is the Kalash), who live in three steep but fertile valleys of the Hindu Kush on the border between Pakistan and Afghanistan. The Kafirs are a remarkable people, who appear at one time to have ruled the whole of Chitral. The numerous mysteries surrounding them have drawn scholars and travellers from all over the world to their little country. The Kafirs are pagans, probably the only pagans still left in this part of the world. They worship in exotic temples. They wear strange clothes. Entering Kafiristan was like penetrating into a totally unknown world.

The most remarkable thing about the Kafirs is their claim to be descended from a small band of soldiers who deserted the armies of Alexander the Great when he crossed these mountains to establish his claim to the empire of the Achaemenids. Like many before me—and, as it turned out, with an equal lack of success—I went to Kafiristan to discover whether I could in any way substantiate this extraordinary legend.

I also went there for another reason. The Kafirs still have a vital tradition of folk art. Their temples and many of their houses are adorned with charming, intricate carvings. Their domestic utensils are also highly decorated. Even more important, however, are the life-sized wooden statues which are erected near the tombs of the dead. I was anxious to acquire some examples of Kafir art, and above all one of the grave statues. The Political Agent in Chitral kindly supplied me with a native policeman to accompany me as a guide and translator—and also to encourage the Kafirs to sell me any objects I might wish to buy.

We set up camp in the village of Brun. My policeman brought me a rapid succession of visitors, all of whom I questioned closely about Kalash traditions. No important clues emerged from these interviews though I did succeed in learning much of interest. I came to be especially intrigued by the burial customs of the Kafirs. Why were several women buried together in one coffin? Why did only men have the privilege of a coffin to themselves? Why was a man's death regarded as an occasion for celebration? What was the function of the very stylized grave statues?

The answers I received to these questions were all clearly evasive. From them, however, I managed to piece together one significant fact about the grave statues. They were placed in the village burial ground, one year after a man's death. They were not protected by any form of paint or varnish from the severe weather so that they rapidly decayed and rotted away. This was done intentionally, for the Kafirs believed that only when a man's grave statue has disintegrated was his soul finally set free.

This discovery unsettled me. Now that I had seen these statues I was more determined than ever before to acquire one. They were of considerable ethnological interest and I wished to bring back one of them for the Pitt-Rivers Museum in Oxford.

But would it be fair to do so? I did not myself hold the Kafir superstition, but I knew that it was real enough for them. Would it not be brutal and insensitive, therefore, to steal one of their statues and have it preserved for ever in the purified air of an English museum where it would never rot away, and never give the soul of the dead man the freedom which was its due?

But the collector's greed is usually more powerful than his conscience.

I rid my mind of any scruples, chose a statue and sent the policeman to negotiate for its purchase with the dead man's family. They were, of course, reluctant to part with it; but in this land the policeman's authority and behind him that of the Political Agent—could not be resisted, and there was nothing for the family to do except to demand the highest price they could think of. They finally parted with the statue for fifty rupees, that is £4.

I was anxious for the statue to be sent on to the airstrip at Chitral immediately, as I did not want to be bothered with it for the remainder of my stay in Kafiristan. We accordingly summoned the local carpenter, who within a few hours made a large box to hold the statue. I tied a rope round it, wrote my name and address in Urdu on the lid, and paid a stout young Kafir, a relative of the dead man, ten rupees to carry it to the airline office in Chitral.

When I returned the following week to Chitral I learnt from the Mess Subardar what had happened next. Unfortunately, when the Kafir arrived with the box at the airline office, he pointed to my name on the lid and said that *I* was inside. I had been killed in an accident, he reported. The Political Agent, was at once informed, a sorrowful telegram dispatched to my family and, if the Mess Subardar was to be believed, the whole town of Chitral plunged into mourning.

The following day my "coffin" (on which I had had the rare privilege of writing my own name) was prepared for the flight to the plains. Now the Chitral airstrip is situated at a height of more than 6,000 feet. Consequently all cargo and indeed all passengers have to be carefully weighed, and the distribution of weight in the plane precisely arranged, before take-off.

When my "coffin" was placed on the scales it was found to weigh a mere 150 lbs. It so happens that I weigh rather more than that, and with the wood of the packing case, the overall weight should have been at least 200 lbs.

Sensing that something was wrong, the airline man sent an urgent report to the Political Agent to say that only part of my body had been sent out from Kafiristan. He feared that perhaps I had been decapitated, or my limbs were missing. Would he kindly come with the Agency Surgeon to open the coffin?

A nervous crowd gathered in the airline office. The surgeon arrived. He prised the lid open . . .

Is there anything more to tell? The Kafir had had his revenge. I felt he was entitled to it.

Sketching Episode

by Olga Collett

I WAS NEW to the Colony. Hong Kong was—perhaps still is—a most beautiful place with its islands and sampans coming and going, and wooded hillsides, looking surprisingly Scottish, on the mainland behind Kowloon. So I took sandwiches, my sketch book, and a fistful of pencils, and hopped a Kowloon bus for a day in the country. Beyond the last bus-stop I walked for about an hour, then left the road to follow a stream which promised a small waterfall higher up. It was an ideal place for lunch and for a landscape drawing afterwards. I was delighted when a group of half a dozen Chinese arrived on the other side of the stream. They chattered in their thin high-pitched Chinese voices and splashed extremely dirty feet in the stream. I made some quick drawings of this enchantingly new subject. Soon they saw me, and silence fell. Presently they came across to my side of the stream.

I am only too familiar with the curiosity that drives anyone in the neighbourhood of an artist at work to move in to stare at what is going on. But I did wish that this lot hadn't moved in quite so enthusiastically. They began to touch my fingers, my ears, my hair. Then I remembered that the hotel amah had seemed fascinated in much the same way with my clothes and my hairdo, so I entered into the spirit of the thing and showed them how my shoelaces did up and got my handkerchief out of my pocket for them to pass from hand to hand. A good time was being had by all. They began urging me to go along with them, pointing upstream towards the little waterfall. I thought they wanted to show it to me, and obligingly got up to go along.

At this point my sketch book fell to the ground open at a drawing I had made of one of them. I picked it up and showed it to the one who had hold of my arm. He let go of me to take the book. Then it was pandemonium. They all talked at once, pointing at me, at the book, at the one who was the subject of my sketch. I grabbed one of them, planted him a few paces away in front of me and began to draw him. Half an hour later, five out of the six were clutching portrait sketches of themselves, and, rather bored by it all by now, I was just embarking on the sixth. Then, to my complete amazement, a very English, and a very quietly angry voice behind me said, "And just what the hell do you think you're doing?" It immediately went on to tell me to turn around and begin walking slowly back to the road, did I understand, at once please. Okay, so I recognized authority when I heard it. I went round my now withdrawn and silent group of portrait models, giving each one a pencil as a souvenir, and saying idiotic social things like, "Well, sorry, I have to go now, thanks for sitting for me." I think I even said, "Be seeing you. . . ." We reached the road, and I was waved into the sidecar of a motor-bicycle standing there. Seconds later we were on our way back to the city. As we rounded the corner I glanced back. My friends were staring after us. Suddenly something told me that this had been no picnic after all, that I had had a very narrow escape from some unimaginably horrible experience.

My Chinese friends, as I had thought them, were a well-known and particularly nasty lot of roving Chinese bandits who, if my wedding ring had been gold, would immediately have cut my finger off to get it. But, as it happens, it is platinum, and platinum, to a Chinese, looks like silver, which has no value to them. Also I wasn't wearing ear rings and had no jade pins in my hair. Then, in my ignorance, no bravery about it, just plain ignorance, I hadn't appeared afraid which would have stampeded them, and then, too, I'd caught their interest and vanity with my drawings. But I really owed my escape to the bus conductor. He'd told his brother-in-law in the Kowloon police about the white woman who had gone walking off his bus into bandit-infested country. The brother-in-law had alerted the police-station, and, fortunately for me, the British head policeman had decided the story was worth investigating.

So I was lucky. All I lost was six drawing pencils. I might have lost my finger. I might even have lost my life.

Washing Hands in Strange Places

by Nina Epton

ONE OF MY very proper Scottish aunts, who was secretly rather horrified that I should travel so much alone and interview "so many *men*", plucked up enough courage one day to ask me: "Nina, I've often wondered, how do you—er—*wash your hands* in all those strange places you go to?" My immediate reaction was to exclaim: "Thank you, Aunt Hannah! What a good idea for a title: 'Washing hands in strange places'. I must use it some time."

My earliest memory of unusual toilets is at my kindergarten school in Derbyshire, when all the pipes froze and our worried headmistress arranged a row of potties behind a screen; the sort that occasionally crop up at country sales, very large, with scalloped edges, and highly decorated. "Which one did *you* choose?" we whispered excitedly to one another. "I chose the pink one with the cherries painted on it." . . . "I chose the blue one with the wild roses." . . . We were quite sorry when the thaw came.

A couple of years later, in Paris, I was knocked down by a bicycle in front of a café. Much to my confusion, the excited witnesses, men and women, shouted to my parents, in French of course, "Take her to the toilet—take her to the toilet—one must always go after a fright." I was shoved into a cubicle without a seat and two giant footprints, in concrete, one each side of a shallow china bowl in the floor . . . so low that when I pulled the chain the water overflowed. This experience frightened me much more than the accident.

With experiences such as these (and there were many more) behind me you might think that when I embarked on my wider travels in after years I would be prepared for all eventualities. Not at all! Until then, my experiences had been solitary ones. Now I was to be confronted with having to perform in public . . . an inhibiting experience if ever there was one. It happened in Morocco.

I'd been spending the day outside the beautiful old city of Fez, in a village of tiny whitewashed Arab houses surrounded by palm trees where —to quote Aunt Hannah—I had been interviewing "a lot of men". In the evening, before the long drive back to Fez, I intimated to one of my French-speaking hosts that I would like to "wash my hands", so would he please take me to the women's quarters? He looked a little apprehensive, I thought, as he beckoned me to follow him to the back of the house where the women and children were assembled.

My wishes were conveyed to them by my host who then disappeared, leaving me in their charge. The women began to bustle round me in a frenzy of activity: one servant ran to the charcoal fire to fetch hot water from a cauldron, another scampered off to find a handsome silver jug, one child brought a bar of pink scented soap from a cupboard and placed it on a little silver platter, another brought out a towel, while in the rear yet another servant proceeded to light a huge lantern.

All these operations were directed by the Commander of the harem, glittering and clinking in an ankle-length blue muslin dress and gold-embroidered belt, long golden earrings, bangles galore and a necklace as big as a breastplate. But what—I began to wonder—had all these activities to do with my original request? It looked very much as though the women had understood that I did—literally—want to "wash my hands".

The Commander shouted at me in Arabic. Seeing that her words didn't register, she then pushed me towards a narrow flight of steps leading to the flat roof and made a wide scooping gesture. Up we all went—pre-ceded by the servant with the lantern—making enough noise to rouse all the neighbours and cause them to focus their penetrating Arab eyes on to our small roof terrace. Could the toilet be up here? There wasn't any sign of one. . . . The Commander of the harem, her children and her servant, stood round me in a ring. Then the servant carrying the jug of water took two steps forward, the Commander took another two and held out a towel. . . . At last, the penny dropped, this roof was the "ladies" and they were waiting for me to perform. I was so taken aback that I reacted in a manner which appeared bizarre both to my audience and even to myself. I seized the proffered jug and carefully sprinkled the water in a circle in the middle of the terrace. Why, they obviously wanted to know, was the strange English lady doing this? Was it perhaps a ritual performed in the West, a kind of sympathetic magic such as rain makers use. Why, indeed, *was* I doing this? I asked myself. Probably to gain time, to brace myself for the ordeal, although by now I was so inhibited that nothing could or would happen. How disappointing it was for everybody.

Another awkward incident which I recall with amusement, although it didn't seem funny at the time, took place in a Javanese village where I had gone to study peasant life, and live in a bamboo hut with a family of five. There was no furniture and we all slept gregariously on a bamboo mat placed on a wooden frame. As I took off my clothes under my nylon dressing-gown (to the astonishment of my hosts who didn't bother to remove their sarongs at night) I reflected that it was a good thing I never had to get up during the night. How awkward it would be, with so many people around, to rise and disturb them all, grope in the dark for the latch —there was no electricity of course, and stumble out into the darkness.... But supposing that, just for once, I *did* feel like getting up? This unfortunate thought preyed on my mind to such an extent that it ended by producing the very effect I dreaded. So, for once in my life, I had to get up in the middle of the night, thereby causing the family disturbance I had anticipated. It was no use my trying to protest: the whole family rolled off the bamboo mat, one by one, to come to my assistance ... people are so hospitable in the East.

The eldest daughter lit a coconut-oil lamp, the smaller children opened the front door, while the parents sat expectantly on the edge of the bamboo-mat-bed. I glided rapidly out of the house and made unsteadily for a clump of jungly foliage. When the eldest daughter, who was holding up the lamp for me in the doorway, saw me wandering off so far she gave a little cry of alarm, ran after me and dragged me back, indicating that I should make myself comfortable in front of the house. Shades of Aunt Hannah! I just couldn't bring myself to comply, so I stumbled on stubbornly towards the stream that encircled the village. I tried to make the girl understand that I didn't want her to follow me, but it was no use. I broke into a run, the girl ran after me and a ludicrous midnight chase ensued in and out of the palm trees. I began to hear voices from neighbouring bamboo huts ... no doubt they were beginning to think a burglar —or perhaps even a dangerous animal—was prowling through their peaceful village. It was really quite absurd of me. I suppose a psychiatrist would say I'd been conditioned in my infancy. Things were so much simpler and more natural in the jungle!

My latest exotic experience was a couple of years ago in Japan where—in the rural areas—I found again the old "giant footsteps" of my early Parisian days, except that the footprints were more petite. The Japanese, who like to see beauty everywhere, provided tasteful flower arrangements even there. One of my Zen Buddhist hosts assured me that it was a good place to practise *zazen*-deep meditation, but I never got to that stage and I doubt whether I ever shall. No, I don't see myself combining metaphysics with "washing my hands". I must still be too Western.

Rama The Wolf Boy

by Glen Thomas

IT WAS ABOUT two years before I left India in 1950 that I had the most unforgettable experience of my life. I was seventeen at the time and was spending my school holidays with my father, a retired Civil Servant, my mother and two brothers in Chunar, a small town near Mirzapur in the United Provinces of India (now known as Uttar Pradesh).

One evening my father remarked that an old friend of his, a Mr. Jackson, would be arriving the next day and would probably stay for a week at our house.

Mr. Jackson turned out to be a retired officer of the Indian Army, a big jolly man, well over six feet tall and he must have weighed at least twenty stones. Although he was over sixty years of age, he was very energetic and youthful in appearance.

After dinner he held us all enthralled with his travelling and hunting experiences and my two brothers and I enthusiastically agreed to his proposal that we should accompany him on a shooting expedition the following day.

The morning air was cool and fresh and we made good progress over the rough scrub-land surrounding the town. We soon reached the jungle and after about two hours of slow travel we came to an area of smoother ground in which there was a little village. Mr. Jackson who spoke Hindustani fluently, asked the headman his advice about likely places to find the wild boar and deer which abound in these parts, and also arranged to have the help of some of his men on a pre-arranged signal with rifle shots, the sound of which carries for miles in the still air.

Refreshed after the short rest, we again set out through more difficult country. By midday the heat was intense and although we had covered quite a distance we had not encountered any game.

By this time my brothers and I were tired of the whole thing and would have liked to go back. Suddenly, however, our hopes were raised as our leader peered intently through his field glasses and motioned us to move forward cautiously. Mr. Jackson again looked through the glasses. Suddenly he stiffened, then turned to us with a look of surprise on his face and said, "It's a pack of wolves and there seems to be a large monkey playing with them." One does not usually associate monkeys with wolves and we decided to investigate.

Once more we moved forward until we were about fifty yards from the pack. Cautiously Mr. Jackson peered through the long grass. Then he gave a gasp. "Have a look with the binoculars and tell me what you see." I did as he asked and was astonished to see that what we had previously thought was a monkey was actually a young man, hopping about on all fours with the wolves.

My brothers, Charles and Allan, had a look and confirmed that it was indeed a young man.

All thoughts of looking for game were forgotten and we decided to try and catch the Wolf Boy. We separated as quickly as possible and at a signal from our leader we all rushed forward yelling loudly.

The boy and three of the wolves crashed past me and I shouted to my companions to follow me. We bulldozed our way through the thick undergrowth and trees, heedless of cuts and bruises, but try as we might, we soon lost sight of our quarry and had to resort to tracking. After about an hour the tracks led us to a deep hole in the ground. It was an animal trap of the kind used to catch large animals which step on the false cover and fall in. When we looked down we saw the Wolf Boy cowering against the side.

The problem now was how to get him out. After some thought, Mr. Jackson decided to retrace our tracks for some distance and then fire four shots in the air, as a signal to the villagers to send us help, as previously arranged. Charles, Allan and I sat down to wait.

It seemed hours before our leader returned with four strapping villagers. They didn't seem to share our excitement at all and gave the impression that they were carrying out nothing more than routine work. Their equipment consisted of a strong net with four ropes tied to the corners, two long bamboo poles and some loose extra ropes.

They let the net carefully down into the hole and by pushing the boy with one of the long poles eventually got him to step on to it. Then the ropes were quickly pulled together and the net drawn up. When this operation was completed, the men immediately wrapped the net tightly round the boy who was struggling wildly and secured him with more ropes. The net was then slung on to the bamboo poles and in this crude manner we conveyed him back to the village where we engaged four more men to help us with the final stage of our journey back to Chunar.

We left the village in the evening equipped with lanterns and had a nerve-racking return through the woods in the darkness which falls very suddenly in this latitude.

We eventually arrived home at 11 p.m. and were met by my anxious parents who were, of course, amazed to see the results of our expedition.

We now had to decide where to put the boy for the night. He couldn't be left bound, and he could easily have escaped from a room. I suddenly remembered a large cage which had been used for hens lying in an outhouse. It was strong and had a padlock on the gate. We decided it would have to do. After provisioning it with food and water, the Wolf Boy was put in and the net was snipped off him from the outside, and so we left him.

Charles, Allan and I were up early the following morning and had our first proper look at the captive. He was a youth of about eighteen years of age and looked as though he would be fairly tall if he stood upright. His hair was long and shaggy and some of it covered his face, but through it we could see that, like most Indians, his features were fine and he had beautiful dark eyes and remarkably strong teeth. He breathed heavily and we noticed that his body was covered with scars, probably received in fights with the wolves over food.

We watched fascinated as he prowled round the cage on all fours like a wild tiger. We tried to feed him by hand but he snapped at our fingers instead of the food. For two days we persevered trying him with all kinds of food, but apart from milk and water he would take nothing.

This began to worry us as his condition was deteriorating and we were afraid he would die of starvation. We eventually had to accept the offer of a Mr. and Mrs. Smith, a couple who had had a great deal of experience in taming wild animals, to take him to their home in Mirzapur.

After a week with them Rama, as they called him, began to improve. They fed him for a month on raw meat and then began gradually cooking it more and more until after eight months he was eating normal food.

At first the call of the wild was strong and he would howl like a wolf every evening, but he soon began to settle down and in the comfort and protection of his new home lost his desire to return to the jungle.

When he had gained the boy's confidence, Mr. Smith began teaching him to walk and talk. This required a great deal of patience and perseverance. For a long time he walked on his toes with his knees bent. Teaching him to speak was also very difficult. He would listen carefully and tried hard to speak, but it was about eighteen months before he was able to form his words clearly.

It was, of course, impossible to find out where Rama came from originally or how he came to be living in the wild with the wolf-pack. It is, however, thought that a she-wolf, probably having lost her litter, would be quite capable of prowling round an Indian village at night and carrying off a young baby, or perhaps a woman gathering firewood in the forest might give birth to her child and possibly die, in which case a she-wolf would not kill the baby but take it as her own.

The amazing thing is that a child could grow to maturity in the care of such wild foster-parents in a country where, in spite of all their human parents' efforts, growing up for many children is still a very hard struggle against malnutrition and poverty.

BIRDS AND
BEASTS

The Wandering Albatross

by Admiral Sir William Jameson

A FAMOUS ORNITHOLOGIST once wrote, "I now belong to the higher cult of mortals, for I have seen the albatross." And that goes for me too. It was like this.

I was serving in the aircraft carrier *Ark Royal*. Late in November 1939 we were in the South Atlantic, hunting for the German pocket battleship *Graf Spee*. She'd sunk a ship in the Indian Ocean, off Madagascar, but the Admiralty thought she might double back into the South Atlantic to raid the valuable traffic from South America. We were ordered to patrol south of the Cape of Good Hope, on the edge of that stormy area around Antarctica known as the Roaring Forties.

We'd been at sea for a long time with nothing to look at except empty ocean. There was no news and life was monotonous. Suddenly a great, white bird appeared. It skimmed across the waves, turned into the wind, soared up to forty or fifty feet, banked towards the ship and swooped down at high speed to pass across our wake. The *Ark* was steaming at seventeen knots, but the albatross, gliding on apparently motionless wings and covering much more ground than we were, seemed to have no difficulty in keeping up with us. It was quite fearless, sometimes coming within a few feet of the flight deck and staring back at us. Sometimes it would settle briefly on the water, to gobble up scraps thrown overboard from the galley. At nightfall it was still with us. Next morning we were further south. The sky was grey. The wind was strong and "our" albatross had been joined by several others.

The glass was falling and soon it was blowing a gale. These waters are some of the stormiest in the world and the sea was spectacular, with waves thirty or forty feet high and three or four hundred yards from crest to crest. With the ship pitching and rolling all our aircraft were grounded, but the albatrosses were enjoying themselves, swooping around at high speed, soaring, diving within an inch or two of the spume-covered sea; perfectly at home and moving in any direction they wished. Wedged in a sheltered corner of the lurching deck I watched them for hours. I shall never forget it.

There are several things about the Wandering Albatross which make it unique amongst birds. Its long, narrow wings are enormous, often over ten feet from tip to tip. Aerodynamically they are beautifully shaped, for this great bird, weighing as much as a farmyard goose, is a glider. It hardly ever flaps its wings, relying on eddies and up-currents to remain airborne. Most birds fly only intermittently, but the albatross, except in the rare calms, spends its life in the air. Sleep, as we know it, seems unnecessary. Its flight is so effortless it can rest in the air, as a trout, keeping its place in a stream, can rest in running water. When it alights to pick up its natural food, cuttlefish and squids and the small shrimps known as "krill", it uses its enormous wings to get aloft again simply by spreading them. The wind does the rest, wafting it from a wave-top into the air.

Albatrosses must, of course, come ashore to lay their eggs and rear their young. They breed on half a dozen remote islands such as South Georgia, Kerguelen and Campbell Island. There the wind blows half a gale for most of the year and they can get airborne by waddling into it and laboriously flapping their great wings, for they're rather helpless creatures out of their own element.

They live for fifty or sixty years and are slow developers. After an elaborate courtship ceremony a single egg is laid which takes more than two months, seventy-two days, to hatch out. This is in March, with the severe sub-Antarctic winter just beginning. The chick remains in the nest for at least another six months. It is fed by one or other parent, though at increasingly long intervals which may extend to three weeks, until it leaves the nest and forages for itself.

Learning to fly is a laborious process. The youngsters waddle up a hill, launch themselves clumsily into the air, and often go base over beak when they land again. Eventually they master the art, and off they go to sea.

For the next few years (no one knows exactly how long this adolescent period lasts) the young albatrosses remain at sea, usually in the air and nearly always out of sight of land. Their plumage gradually changes, from the sombre brown in which they left home to the beautiful black and white dress of maturity. When they are three to four years old, sex begins to call. They are not as yet ready for mating, but the young birds now come back with the older, nesting birds in the Antarctic autumn to the island where they were hatched, and indulge in some preliminary frolics. At four or five, matters become serious. They pair off, with each other or with older birds, build one of the low mounds of mud and tussock grass which serve as nests, or repair an old one, and start procreating on their own.

As parent birds are occupied for some ten months with brooding and feeding their young they're ready for a holiday when the next autumn comes round. So off they go to sea for a year, returning to breed again in the following autumn, thus producing an egg every two years.

Wandering Albatrosses are monogamous, but whether they stick to the same partner is doubtful. Probably, like humans, some do, and some don't. Knowledge about such details is gradually being assembled, but a bird which is normally only seen in the ocean wastes or on rarely visited islands is not an easy subject for ornithologists. However, exceptionally, a great many do spend a few weeks off the coast of New South Wales at certain seasons, feeding on the offal carried out to sea from Sydney's slaughter houses. A party led by two pen-friends of mine, Doug Gibson and Bill Lane, has for some years past caught and ringed a number of these birds. Several of them have been recovered on nesting sites in South Georgia, the other side of the world, by another friend of mine, Lance Tickell, and birds ringed by him have been caught off New South Wales. The fact that they make this great journey is therefore scientifically established.

Wandering Albatrosses must cover tremendous distances each year. Our first *Ark Royal* wanderer was with the ship for over a thousand miles, circling round and flying at least twice this distance in three days. A hundred thousand miles a year through the air wouldn't be a fanciful estimate.

Albatrosses have always had a special attraction for mariners, coming out of nowhere in the loneliest parts of the southern oceans, remaining with ships for days on end and then as suddenly making off on their own affairs. Their size, fearlessness of man, effortless flight and sheer beauty would have been enough to make them remarkable. They are also a fabulous bird, and I suppose that some of you, like me, struggled at school with Coleridge's *Rime of the Ancient Mariner*. You remember,

"God save thee, ancient Mariner,
From the fiends, that plague thee thus!
Why look'st thou so?"
—"With my crossbow
I shot the Albatross"—

and so on.

Well, when I was writing a little book about these birds, I went to the British Museum to trace down the origin of the superstition that killing an albatross brought bad luck. The result of my researches was unexpected. I found sailors in the eighteenth and early nineteenth century had not the slightest objection to catching and killing the birds, making tobacco pouches out of their feet, muffs for their girl-friends from the soft breast feathers, paper-clips of their beaks, and other fanciful objects. They even ate them, but only, I think when very hungry, for the flesh is said to be tough and strongly flavoured. How then did the superstition arise? The poet himself invented it.

In the autumn of 1797 Coleridge, with his friend Wordsworth and Wordsworth's sister Dorothy, set off on a walking tour along the Quantock Hills. Their funds were very low and, to defray the costs of the expedition, Coleridge and Wordsworth decided to write a poem. Coleridge mentioned how another friend, a certain Mr. Cruikshank, had dreamt of a phantom ship, manned by skeletons. Wordsworth suggested that some crime should have been committed aboard, bringing spectral persecution. A few days earlier he had been reading a book from his library published in 1757, *A Voyage Round The World by The Great South Sea* by Captain George Shelvocke, in which the shooting of an Albatross is described.

"Suppose," said Wordsworth, "you represent him (the Ancient Mariner) as having killed one of these birds on entering the South Sea, and the tutelary spirits of these regions take upon them to revenge the crime."

Coleridge, his imagination thoroughly stimulated, now took over, and the *Rime* as it eventually appeared in 1798 was entirely his own.

> And I had done a hellish thing,
> And it would work 'em woe:
> For all averr'd I had killed the bird
> That made the breeze to blow.
> Ah wretch! said they, the bird to slay,
> That made the breeze to blow!

Cats, Cats, All the Way

by E. B. Chapman

CATS. YOU EITHER hate 'em or you love 'em. I love 'em. I always have and I always shall. My mother, God rest her, couldn't abide 'em.

"I don't think we want pussy in the same house, dear," she would say, and all my tearful, little-boy rebelliousness couldn't move her. She just didn't like cats.

So I kept my cat box in the cycle shed. It was comfortably padded out with old, woollen underwear, and there was a large tin of kitchen scraps nearby.

I suppose it wasn't an ideal arrangement, but it worked well enough. I entertained a string of strays, who came again and again—and not, I maintain, just because they knew which side their bread was buttered—and Mother, bless her heart, pretended none of this was happening.

Then I left home and found a girl who also loved cats and married her.

There were three of us from the start. Tanza, a tabby, had no pedigree —what's a pedigree, anyway?—but she was without doubt a lady. She could be friskily playful or purringly quiescent, taking her cue from us. She would talk to us all the time with a wealth of facial expression, but I loved her best for the way she could share a companionable silence.

Several years and many kittens later, Tanza died, and the twins Toots and Rufus were sent to console us.

Life with the new kittens became one long romp. Both were huskily male and athletically disposed. Clap your hands, and they would hurl themselves into your arms. Call a greeting, and one or the other—sometimes both—would be on your shoulder nuzzling your ear. Yet they were, as all cats are, as individual as people.

And, like people, they had their problems.

One day, our small daughter, Patricia, came home with a suspicious-looking brown-paper bag. My wife looked in, shuddered, and said: "I don't think we want a tortoise in the house, dear." Patricia wept bitterly. The cats sniffed delicately at the new arrival. After a while, my wife began muttering, "I don't know what the things eat, anyway." Patricia, scenting victory, flung her arms around her mother's neck and said: "You are a darling, darling, Mummy."

All was peace again. But the cats were in trouble.

You couldn't really blame Crawler, as we christened the tortoise. He just wanted to be friendly, and anyway he was curious. A vegetarian himself, he probably tipped up the saucers of milk and clawed his way through the plates of cat food just for the hell of it. But gradually Crawler became accepted as one of the family, and eventually the cats learned to take his tank-like method of locomotion in their stride. He moved in straight lines, and if they were in the way he tended to go over rather than around them.

This strange ménage—two cats and a tortoise—became a local legend. Then, within a month, Crawler and Rufus were no more. Crawler went peacefully; Rufus, tragically.

One day, slipping downstairs to make the early morning tea, I opened the kitchen door and stumbled into a solid wall of coal gas. The baleful hissing ceased as I turned off the tap. Holding my breath, I pulled open the outside door and staggered into the garden. Looking back, I could see Rufus, his fur strangely wet and matted, stretched stiffly on the floor.

Later we reconstructed what must have happened. Prowling the slippery rim of the gas copper, Rufus must have skidded into the yielding mass of washing left in soak overnight and knocked the gas tap on as he scrambled out.

Patricia was heartbroken. Rufus had been her favourite. We tried to comfort her. We daren't tell her that we ourselves had been in danger.

Anyway, we still had Toots. It was lucky for him he chose that night to look up his lady friend.

Life went on, and then one day Patch arrived dramatically. He was found, like Moses in the bullrushes, when my wife took a torch to see who had left a crying baby in the front garden. She came in cradling a kitten and saying that some brute must have frightened it. We learned later the kitten had been flung from a speeding bus after a gang of youths, who had promised to find it a home, had tired of teasing it.

Patch rallied on a diet of brandy and white of egg. The vet said his heart was permanently weakened, but Little Patch grew into Big Patch and outlived the sedate and dignified Toots who died peacefully in his bed at the ripe old age of sixteen.

It was not the same without Toots. We all felt it—my wife; Patricia, home from college for the summer vacation; myself and, again and markedly so, the surviving pet. Patch, in fact, started to die himself when he lost Toots, the only real "mother" he had known. In a matter of months, the vet was telling my wife that Patch had had a good life in a comfortable home; that now it would be kindest to put him to sleep.

I came home that day to the milk saucer, the food plate and the wicker sleeping-basket that no longer had any meaning. We looked at one another. We knew we couldn't face this kind of thing again. Patch, because of our early struggle to save him and because of his almost human gratitude and affection, was a favourite and pampered son. The house seemed strange without a cat for the first time in over thirty years. But it seemed better to leave it that way.

So for both of us life lost a dimension, as it does for all creatures when the young leave the nest. Coming down to a cold emptiness in the darkness of a winter morning was hard to bear.

Then in the tradition of the best-loved fairy stories, it happened.

A cardboard box was on the front doorstep when my wife fetched the morning milk. We noticed a screw of paper tucked into the securing cord as I carried it through to the lighted kitchen. I put it down carefully as my wife read it out, "Please give me a home. My name is Monty."

We listened: there wasn't a sound. I loosened the cord and raised the lid. Flanked by a saucer of cereal and milk and an unopened tin of cat food was the smallest tabby kitten I had ever seen. Blue eyes, saucer-big and infinitely trusting, looked up at us.

You can guess the rest.

I just don't think cat lovers are ever meant to be without cats. For them life is intended to be a matter of cats, cats, all the way.

My Dog Finnigan

by Elizabeth Sheppard-Jones

I ALWAYS SUSPECT those people who write about dogs; it is so easy to become dangerously sentimental, and I personally hate to hear that oft quoted phrase "the more I see of humans, the better I like my dog". This is utter rubbish for there is no dog, however remarkable, the equal of any human being, however nondescript. That said, I shall now tell you about Finnigan, who is extraordinarily beautiful, not particularly intelligent, being somewhat soft in the head or, as we say in Wales, a little bit "twp", and certainly far removed from being human; but he is my dog, I do like him, and I should like you to like him, too.

Finnigan is a Shih Tzu—and if your reaction to this bit of information is the same as most people who meet him for the first time—you will be exclaiming at this moment: "A She what?" The fact that he looks as if his mother might have been a Peke who ran off with an old English sheep-dog does not make him any less of an aristocrat. I repeat, he is a Shih Tzu, a Tibetan dog, a Lion Dog of Buddha, whose forefathers have been bred in China for the last two hundred years, and whose forefathers before that turned the prayer-wheels in the lamaseries of Tibet. These dogs have long silky hair—Finnigan's is white and honey in colour—and a waterfall of this hair showers down over their eyes: it is the custom to tie up this in a rubber-band, like a miniature pony tail, to reveal the rather lovely large brown eyes. But there is a legend which says that when a Dalai Lama dies, his soul resides temporarily in the bodies of these small animals until he is born again. The long hair, it seems, ensures that the Dalai Lama's soul stays in peace and shadow, allowing him to sleep undisturbed. Judging by the behaviour of Finnigan, all I can say is that it would be a foolish Dalai Lama who chose to reside in him. True, he has his moments of contemplation but they are few and far between and, as far as I can judge, are not spent in contemplating his navel but in careful consideration of what wickedness he can next get up to.

Of course, he should never really have been called Finnigan—and he is surely the only Eastern potentate with an Irish name. Most Shih Tzus rejoice in splendidly exotic names like Choo-choo and Yu Tse and Yang Ping; and many of their names have wonderful English meanings like Prosperity, Child of Jade, Flower Petal, Happiness, Heart of Lion, and it is a bit of a come-down to have Finnigan added to this poetic list. But, really, I had no choice. I have a young nine-year-old boy friend called Sean Finnigan and a few weeks before the arrival of the puppy, Sean was due to move with his family to London. This parting was a blow both to him and to me, and when he came to bid me goodbye, he asked if I would do something for him. "Anything," I said. "So that you won't never ever forget me?" he said. "But I couldn't, I wouldn't forget you," I replied. "You might, people do," was his wise answer. "But if you named the puppy after me, you'd be bound to remember me, wouldn't you?" Who could resist such a plea? I certainly couldn't—and Finnigan it was.

Finnigan is much admired, not only because he is very pretty but also because he is a rare breed and the only Shih Tzu certainly in the area where I live. I was in my invalid tricycle the other day, with him on my knee—parked outside the cleaners actually—when a strange man approached me, a sailor recently come into Cardiff docks I guessed by his rolling gait and the fact that he was not very sober, even though it was only early afternoon. "Lovely little dog you got there, lady," he said, breathing alcoholic fumes over me, and nearly asphyxiating Finnigan. He made a great fuss over the dog and Finnigan made quite a fuss of him and then the sailor transferred his attentions to me. Jerking his thumb towards a pub on the opposite corner, he invited both of us to have a pint with him. "I'll carry you in," he promised. "Nothing to fear." I was very tempted to accept; it would have been quite a sight for the afternoon shoppers in the High Street of our small quiet town—Finnigan and I crossing the road in the arms of an amiable drunk and disappearing into the Boar's Head. But I refused; he was so unsteady on his feet and I didn't really wish to be dropped in the midst of the busy traffic. However, Finnigan seemed awfully anxious to accept and, a little dubiously, I let him go. The sailor wanted to show him to his mates but when they had disappeared into the Saloon Bar, I began to have qualms. Perhaps I'd never see my dog again. Perhaps he'd be shanghaied. Should I have trusted him to a complete stranger, in spite of the fact that I have the greatest faith in all sailors, drunk or sober? I need not have worried for ten minutes later he was deposited safely back on the pavement by my side. Finnigan smelled of rum and fell over when he wagged his tail. "He refused the beer," said the sailor admiringly, "but tossed off a double rum without blinking." Now, it seems I have on my hands an Eastern dog with an Irish name that has alcoholic tendencies. No wonder he turns up his very snub nose whenever I offer him a dish of Oriental tea!

Aged Parent Meets Horse

---

by J. A. Harrison

ALL HORSES ARE Trojan. Nobody can foresee what they bring with them. If Homer and Virgil and their thousands of commentators had ever had a horse in the family they would have known that the only remarkable fact about their famous horse was that it was made of wood.

My only land is a back garden but my neighbour has five acres of pasture and two Welsh ponies. My daughter rode hired horses from nine years old to seventeen, when she demanded one of her own, "It would be more fun than all our last six holidays put together." While we had nowhere to keep a horse I was safe, but one day she announced the neighbour had said she could keep a horse with his ponies. Over the back-garden wall I told him this was not quite a neighbourly act. He said he knew just how I felt. He had known nothing about it. "These women got talking."

His wife—a lifelong horsewoman—knew where a bay mare was for sale at a reasonable price. She had traded several times with the dealer years ago. Events were moving much too fast for me. I knew nothing about horses and had been told the second-hand car market was simple purity in comparison. In the nearby town I found two acquaintances who lived in the dealer's village and they both gave him a good character, as horse-dealing testimonials go. Another old friend has a son-in-law who is a vet, and I asked if he would examine this mare and hinted that if he rejected it I should not weep very much. I also wondered if I was asking for a high-fee opinion on a low-priced horse. My friend laughed. "I understand perfectly. I've been through it all. Don't worry. I'll tell him what to charge you."

My wife and daughter had seen the horse and liked it. A few days later the vet called and my wife accompanied him to the dealer. He made a full examination and on the return journey said that after a year's careful keeping the animal could probably be sold at a profit, and added that a girl who did not lose the childish passion for horses by her fourteenth birthday never would lose it. He killed my last hope of remaining horse-free.

Betty was delivered a week later. After two years she has shown no real defect. The worst opinion came from the blacksmith—"You nivver get good feet on these blood 'uns." Her quiet brown eyes make it seem wrong to buy and sell her like a car. But, like the Trojan horse, she has captured the city, and family life is different now.

A patch of concrete, about two yards by five, between house and garage, is the saddling enclosure. I understand one does not speak of dressing and undressing a horse. She is led from the fields and the halter attached to a fallpipe, which she will no doubt walk away with one day. The drill is strange. Hooves are picked, cleaned, even varnished and oiled. Her fleece or thatch, or whatever the right term may be, is rubbed with comb and brush, snacks of food are administered with endearing remarks and the concrete is always dirty. I do what I can to serve the new queen but my suggestions are always ignored. One warm day I thought she should be dusted. I was looked at in pity. One wet day she was muddy from rolling in the field, and I offered the use of the car hosepipe. Ignored again. I have suffered for many years from gout, but one day found some of my bandages on Betty. Her ankles showed no signs of gout. I am a specialist on the effects of gout on joints, but have no experience of tails.

There are two sorts of mud—the one on my shoes and the other on riding boots. A speck of mine on the hall carpet is criminal; permanent discoloured patches from the other on the stairs, in the bedrooms and lounge go unreproved. Betty's clothes need as much cleaning as herself.

Normally harness is kept in the garage but, if dirty, in the kitchen or even dining room. Doorknobs are festooned with it and the stink thereof is great even unto the bedrooms. At least half the garage space is now "horse, for the use of". Shelves carry tins and tubes and jars, and the gardening trowels and forks are thrown under a table. It appears female horses have dressing tables like their human counterparts. The floor has a box of carrots, a barrel of turnips, bowls of different sizes, two of what were our best buckets, and, of course, simple dirt.

One of our good towels went under the saddle to prevent a slight rubbing. When winter came, a "New Zealand rug" was needed. I asked how it differed from a British one, having in mind one given to an old uncle when he visited Kaiapoi fifty years ago. I could not see a horse wearing that without sweating. I said I had never seen any of my New Zealand friends wearing rugs and thought the Maoris lived mainly where rugs are not needed. It turned out to be a sort of waterproof jacket fastened to the horse at the neck and rear legs. A perfectly good blanket went as reinforcement under it. The mare rolled in the field just the same, and the bright green rug is now brown. Earlier I had asked why buy a waterproof coat if horses grow winter coats as my daughter had explained. They merely warned that if really bad weather came the animal would occupy the garage because the neighbour's stable holds only his own two. The car would stand outside. I could drain the radiator. I asked if there was no way of draining the horse's radiator, or filling her up with antifreeze. Apparently not, as they ignored me again.

Its main food is not kept in the garage, that is, food apart from grass. A horse eats for about eighteen hours a day. The garage is judged too damp for bran, oats and vitamin "pebbles". This is the grain that lies in the sacks that are kept in the attic of the house that Jack built. And these are the stairs and carpets subject to two trips a day for a bucketful. When the grain merchant delivers in hundred-weight sacks, wife and daughter carry them up to the attic as if it is a privilege. (A week ago a grain merchant's will was proved at £113,000.) The animal also eats apples (sweet only, as befits a lady with a dressing table), brown bread, white bread, currant bread (all preferred buttered), new leaves on rose trees, privet hedge, peas, beans and Christmas trees as and where growing.

One evening Betty did not want to be caught. Both my wife and daughter ran up and down and across that field as I had never seen them run before. They had more colour in their faces than from a month in Majorca. The mare entered into the spirit of the game and eluded them so easily that I laughed and laughed and laughed. Unfortunately I did not bend down behind the wall, and went bottom of the household league. The league is, in this order, horse, cat, daughter, mother, goldfish, me. Sometimes I am above the goldfish, but when one died they nearly sent for the vicar, and I went bottom again.

The actual amount of riding seems far smaller than when a horse was bought at so much per hour. Without anything for depreciation, the distance on the clock must work out at well over five shillings a mile. The yield from the exhaust, which was mentioned to me—an amateur gardener—as so much more valuable than that from a car, is probably good to the owner of the fields, but nil to me. My friends have ceased to suggest that any man who can keep a racing stable can afford to pay for their lunches. Some day they may come round to my idea that I cannot even afford a coffee and ought to be helped. The bitterest remark came from an old rag merchant, a local politician, whom I had not seen for months. He telephoned just before the general election. "I hear you've got a horse . . . (Pause) . . . I did wonder what you'd take up when you retired. . . . And what sort of a cart have you?" And after that he actually asked me to vote Liberal.

After a while catalogues about loose boxes arrived and were left lying where I should see them. I said nothing, except something about seeing a solicitor about rights of way if the garden wall was breached for direct access to the fields. That may have set the owner and groom thinking. After several conferences they suggested that if the gardening equipment could be moved to a shed, for which there was ample room in the back garden, and a four-foot wall built in the garage to divide the car space from the rest, the rest would be big enough for the horse.

And it was so. The shed was creosoted inside and out. When the apples were ready they were gathered and put there. Inside three days they were uneatable as they both smelled and tasted of creosote. All things work together for the good of horses. The mare likes them. If she has offspring she will go down in history for the most valuable breakthrough in breeding—a horse creosoted against damp.

Horses are not animals, or hobbies. They are a religion and most of the worshippers are, as usual, women. They confuse them with babies at times. When Betty does not want to be caught (I laugh behind the door now) she is "Naughty!" and is admonished by taps of one finger on her big bony forehead, plus babytalk. I think TV is also a religion. When I go into the room where the ark of the screen is kept, to disturb their rapt attention is a form of brawling in church. No horse show or race or jumping contest is ever missed by our TV and anyone who talks then is brawling twice over.

Each horse requires two humans as servants and one with a purse. It also requires the kitchen creel for bandages; any or all hooks and door-knobs for harness; the best corner of the floor for saddle; kitchen rug, sink, washbowl and stair carpets for bits of hay, straw and mud; the rest of a kitchen floor for rugs that need drying; a portable radio in the garage to counter loneliness and electric light so that it can distinguish hay from straw; a car with windows for stickers about horse shows, and a back seat for hay, straw, carrots, turnips, loose shoes and anything that is my horse's. Yes, there is a boot, but "chuck it on the back seat—it's quicker."

I am just in from town. My overcoat is wet. I wonder where I dare hang it.

Unarmed Bandit

by James Alan Rennie

FORTY-ODD YEARS AGO I was working as a cowboy "packer" at a famous National Park Hotel in the Canadian Rockies.

One day my particular outfit got back after taking a party of guests on a three-day pony-hike to the timberline and we were amazed to find the hotel seething with excitement and commotion. Plain-clothes detectives and uniformed policemen from as far away as Edmonton were swarming everywhere. It wasn't long before we learned the reason for it all.

Two nights before a wealthy American guest had attended a big dance in the hotel ballroom. When she returned to her private suite, she had placed her jewels on the dressing-table in her bedroom, not troubling to lock them away. Shortly after dawn she was awakened by the sound of her jewel-case falling to the floor, and on getting up to replace it she found it almost empty. Most of her very valuable jewellery had disappeared.

Told this way it sounds a simple enough case of straightforward robbery, but there was more to it than that. In the first place, it was as difficult to discover how the theft had been carried out as it was to uncover the identity of the thief. The results of the police inquiries were very interesting.

Before going to bed the lady had bolted the door and fastened the window of her air-conditioned room. After discovering the loss of her property she found both door and window secured as she had left them. On the face of it, no one could possibly have entered and left the room without her knowledge: yet the jewels were gone.

Among the uniformed men brought in to investigate was the local constable, an ex-member of the Royal Northwest Mounted Police, now serving with the Alberta Provincial Police. The view expressed in the packers' bunkhouse was that if the mystery was to be solved he was the man to do it.

One day I came upon this policeman peering intently at the soil along the borders of a small stream. He was so engrossed that he was unaware of my presence until I pulled up beside him.

"Dropped something?" I asked.

He looked at me with a gleam of excitement in his eyes.

"Nope, guess I've just picked up something," he corrected. "You come right along up here with me."

He led the way to the top of a gentle slope and squatted down behind a juniper bush and motioned me to do likewise.

"Sit quiet and keep your eyes skinned along this bank," he ordered. "If you see anything on the ground move give me a nudge: and I mean just anything."

Still without the foggiest notion of what he was getting at, I did as I was told. Below us the mountain stream warbled between rock and fern at the foot of a narrow, gently-sloping path. So far as I could see, nothing stirred other than the leaping water and the wind-rippled vegetation. Then, during a brief calm, when even the grasses and ferns were stilled, I subconsciously noted that something had moved, though I couldn't tell what. My companion's hand squeezed my knee. My eyes followed his pointing finger. They opened wide when I saw a rounded stone, almost as large as a football, rolling jerkily uphill.

I stared fascinated. The stone appeared to be moving entirely of its own volition. Then, when it reached a point directly beneath me, I saw it was being propelled by a squat, brown animal of a kind I've never seen before. It was standing on its hind legs and pushing relentlessly with its forepaws.

Up and up came the rounded rock until it reached a pile of similar stones half-hidden by tall grasses where it was rolled into a secure position.

"What sort of animal was that?" I asked.

"Pack-rat," was the curt response. "C'mon!"

The constable slid down to the pile of stones. As I joined him I saw a brown, furry creature scurry off through the underbrush. My companion lifted some of the stones and drew tall grasses aside.

"Keeno!" I heard him ejaculate as something flashed in the sun.

We were staring down at a well-lined nest, filled with a most startling array of treasure trove. This ranged from pieces of broken glass and a silver teaspoon to a diamond collar, ear-rings and gem-studded finger-rings. The mystery of the jewel robbery had been solved.

"The pack-rat is as big a thief as any jay," my companion informed me. "When I found a hole in the woman's bedroom floor, close to the waste-pipe under the wash-basin, I figured that here was the explanation for the robbery. Only an insect or a rat could have got into that bedroom, and no insect was big enough to carry off jewellery. After that it was only a matter of finding the pack-rat's cache."

So it was as simple as that! Yet I couldn't help thinking how fortunate that woman was in having a policeman with such a fund of nature lore to carry out investigations on her behalf. Without that knowledge I am sure this baffling mystery would never have been solved, nor would those jewels ever have been seen again.

Terence the Terrapin

by Marie Hamilton

"A TORTOISE!" I said to myself. "Whatever is a tortoise doing down here on the beach?" It was about four inches long, with a flat, not a humped, shell, and was trying to climb the rock towards a trickle of water. "Wait, Terence," I said (the name Terence seemed to suit it). "We will get you a drink and find your owner. You must be someone's lost pet." A bead-like eye regarded me for an instant, then off he went to climb the cliff, only to slither down. So I picked him up. Terence squirmed madly, front and back legs pawing the air, neck outstretched, looking eagerly this way and that. No modest withdrawal beneath the shell, as is usual with the tortoise tribe.

At the greengrocer's I bought the largest lettuce available, and he brought Terence water in a saucer. Between the shop and my house a group of workmen were having their tea break. They scrutinized Terence. "A turtle," they decided, "a small sea-water turtle. It's come all the way from the South Seas. They swim in shoals—they swim in twos. Better go and look for its mate." They told me it was rare for them to come to this country, but it could happen. So it wouldn't be someone's pet. And what did it eat? Not lettuce? No, not lettuce, plankton. Plankton? Yes, plankton. I ask you. What next?

I continued towards my house. When people stopped to admire Terence, he climbed up their arms and round their necks. There were four offers of adoption, though one was called off. After all, a pool would be needed full of salt water and the mysterious plankton, and this I suppose one could only get from the sea itself.

I stopped at the Police Station and there, under the FOUND section Terence was duly registered. I left him with the constable while I telephoned a friend. When I returned I found that the sergeant had whisked Terence down to the Aquarium.

At the Aquarium I found Terence swimming round and round a deep, glass-sided tank, trying in vain to clamber up the sides. The Aquarium owner watched him sadly and said that it was rocks Terence needed, something on to which he could climb. In fact, if he hadn't arrived under police escort, Terence would not have been admitted at all. There was nothing for it but to return Terence to the sea.

With a net on the end of a long pole Terence was fished out of the tank. I walked with him down to a cove fringed with rocks, but my heart felt heavy. I couldn't forget that when I had first found him; he had been trying to *leave* the sea. What if a hungry gull swooped down? Or someone found him who doted on turtle soup? I decided that I simply could not leave him in the cove.

I entered a ship's chandlers. It seemed a suitable sort of place for us to be, and also seemed to bring plankton a little nearer. I put Terence down on the counter. Off he clambered, up a pile of rope. It was getting dark, and what was I to do with this little creature, so full of energy. Then the chandler suggested the zoo! We made inquiries and yes, the zoo manager kindly agreed to accept Terence—next morning.

But where would Terence spend the night? That was easy—in my bath. I hurried home and put Terence in the sink in salt water and with a deep saucer of fresh water in case of thirst. I then lined the bath with newspaper to prevent scratching and arranged rocks from my rock garden in a graduated slope in the centre of the bath. Then I suddenly remembered the plankton. Terence had shown no interest in the large lettuce—and when had he last fed?

Eighty-four steps down to the harbour with my empty bucket and eighty-four back with it full—and I hoped that not *too* many people thought me mad! On my return I found that Terence had climbed right into his saucer of drinking water and was sitting motionless in it. His shell just filled it and for the first time he was quiet and motionless.

After tipping the contents of the bucket into the bath and draping some seaweed over the rocks I transferred Terence. Looking in at 11.15 that night I found him still swimming strongly round and round, ignoring the rocks. I just hoped he'd found the plankton.

Next morning I took Terence to the zoo. "This isn't a tortoise, or a turtle either," said the superintendent, "it's a terrapin, a fresh-water creature, and born, I shouldn't be surprised, in some Italian river. In all probability it arrived in this country by air."

A freshwater creature! No wonder Terence had been so determined to get away from the sea, and had sat in his drinking water. So Terence the terrapin now lives in a pool with a lot of other terrapins. There is a beach and rocks on to which they can climb and sit in the sun, and probably it is all quite like Italy. It amuses me to fancy that I can spot Terence amongst the other terrapins disporting themselves in the pool. For after all, although it was a brief encounter, we had quite a day together. And Terence himself is rather special. It isn't *every* terrapin that comes here by plane, gets lost somehow on a beach, has a ride in a police car and spends the night in a lady's bath.

A BREATH
OF FRESH AIR

Country Callers

by Harry Soan

TAKING THE YEAR through, country people who live in remote places get a surprisingly large and varied number of callers and this doesn't include the baker, grocer or butcher, because many of us aren't served by them. The biggest category are what we class as lost souls. They come up our mountain valley road, find that it terminates in our farmyard and invariably call to inquire where they are. It's difficult to answer them, for we seem to be nowhere in relation to anywhere else.

Next in numbers come the pedlars. We haven't had a gypsy selling pegs for some years now. The last one was a young girl who begged a needle, came back in a few moments asking for cotton, and then, believe it or not, came back again for a button. I told her then that if she returned for a garment to sew it on to, I'd set the dog on her. My family listening from the kitchen spoilt that threat by laughing out loud, because the dog was so peaceable that it would make friends with a rabbit.

The other pedlars that come seem to act on the assumption that all the bright-witted people have gone to live in towns and only the dim-wits have stayed in the country, as easy prey. Men dressed vaguely like seamen come offering us carpets straight off the ship. Others offer lino so violently patterned and brilliantly coloured that you need to shade your eyes when looking at it.

One character we often recall drove on to the yard in a brand new and very large estate car. He bounced out and up to the porch where we were sitting having our after-dinner cup of tea. He declined the offer of a cup, saying he never touched the stuff and from his smart appearance and flash car we concluded that champagne was his usual tipple.

"What are you offering?" I asked.

"Second-hand clothes, sir."

"Who on earth buys second-hand clothes in these affluent times?" I said.

He looked at my patched trousers and ragged jacket and with more frankness than tact, replied "People like you, sir."

"You're wrong," I said. "I wear second-hand clothes, but don't buy them. I get them given me by town relations."

He looked at me as sourly as a striker would look at a blackleg. The look was still on his face when my daughter slipped into the house and whipped out a maternity gown she was reckoning on not needing again. "How much will you give me for this?" she asked.

But he began retreating towards his car. "I'm selling today, lady, not buying." Just then he noticed our neighbour's house across the field. "Who lives over there?" "Lucky folk like us," I said. "They've got town relations, too, who give them clothes." When he got into the car I wished him "Good afternoon", but he didn't reciprocate and I haven't a doubt he thought there ought to be a law against giving old clothes to poor relations on hill farms.

Then there was the Indian in a heavy overcoat and a turban who carried a big suitcase full of silks up the mile-long hill from the village. My wife didn't want anything, but because he looked so disappointed and was yet so polite, she gave him a bob for his trouble. He looked at the bob, then up to heaven and said, "May you be blessed." He bowed gravely and departed. It was like being blessed by an archbishop, she said.

Last year in the early spring, a talkative little man called inquiring for second-hand furniture. My wife, who was dressed up ready to go to town for the weekly shopping, said we had none to spare.

"Ah," he said, "I see it's a holiday cottage you've got here. You've started holidays early this year, haven't you?"

"Holidays?" she queried. "We live here."

"Live here! What all the year round in this godforsaken valley?"

"Yes," she said.

"Blimey missus, I'm real sorry for yer, struth I am."

"Where do you live, then?"

"Cardiff," he said.

"What, all the year round, in a place like that?"

"All right, all right, missus, every man to his taste."

Occasionally in the summer we get people asking if they might camp in the little field by the house. We never refuse, but often wonder what they get out of it when they have transistor radios on so loud and long that they can't so much as hear a bird sing.

But a year or two ago a mother and daughter drove up one June evening in one of those motorized caravans and asked permission to camp. Something about them excited our curiosity and we asked them in for a cup of coffee after supper. The mother was a bright, inquisitive little woman who chattered like a magpie. The daughter was pale, slow-spoken and withdrawn. We learned that next day she was to enter a strictly closed religious order from which, if she were accepted, she'd never emerge again. I thought, rather frivolously, that she might be doing it to get away from her chattering mother, but as we talked I realized that she felt a deep call to this life.

Some time after they had said "Goodnight", I strolled out on to the moonlit yard, and across the field I saw the daughter standing alone by the gate. I've seldom experienced so sad a moment, for it seemed to me she was looking her last on the world and saying "Goodbye" to its life at an age when most are just greeting it.

Living in so remote and quiet a place as our mountain valley, with fewer people in it than there are blackbirds in a garden, means that those who do call on us are seen with a sharpness of focus and experienced with a keenness of taste that more than compensates their fewness in number.

What Price A Tree!

by C. Gordon Glover

A WEASELLY YOUNG man, driving a shrewd-looking little van called at my Essex home the other day for the express purpose of praising my sycamore tree. He knocked on the door, and, when my wife opened it, said that he could not refrain from expressing his admiration of this tree of ours.

Our tree sails like a great green galleon in the summer breezes. At night it is a calling place for owls. Its deep arcades and corridors are a changing interplay of light and shade, and, when the air is humid, its shadows are the meeting place of moths. There is a dove-cote against its trunk. Our white pigeons are perched like bows about its branches, and on summer evenings its perimeter is trimmed with the wings of hunting swallows. When our sycamore tree flowers, the whole garden becomes muzzy with its breath, and our bees, entering into their own, browse in its syrupy pastures and hum in them like uncountable 'cellos.

Since only God, as we know, can make a tree, we feel that He has reason to be well-satisfied with the job He has done on ours. But here was that weaselly young man . . .

"That's a very nice sycamore tree, madam, if I may so—a very nice tree indeed. Very, very nice. As nice a bit of sycamore as ever I saw. Now what about it?"

My wife asked him what about what?

"Come off it, madam, you know as well as I do, there's good money in a tree like that. I don't think you'll quarrel with our prices."

"Money?" gasped my wife. "Prices? *What* prices? What are you talking about?"

"Why—your sycamore. Look, I'll tell you what I'll do—name your figure. If it's okay by you, then it's okay by me. Another thing, my firm doesn't waste no time. A deal's a deal, see? No cheques. Ready cash. Come on—what do you say?"

My wife said nothing. She just began to back away.

"Come on, madam—don't be like that. Look—we do a quick job, and a tidy one, see? Bring all the gear right to the spot. Start right in first thing in the morning. Fetch it down neatly. No mess. Clear up the trimmings, chop it up tidy. Give us four hours, and you'll never know it had been there—well what say?"

"Just this," said my wife, "I shall never forget that you have been here. *Go away.*"

Now That Autumn's Here

by Doreen Anwar

I HAVEN'T BEEN in England in the autumn for twenty years. I sailed for Egypt one blustery March day in 1946, and until now I've never seen the leaves turn to gold. I've been back to England many times, but always in the summer, and I have left, like the swallows, before the autumn. Some expatriates in Egypt get homesick at Christmastime, longing for a sight of a Dickensian Christmas—a white one of course, and carol-singers, and holly and mistletoe and the rest; some long to see the pink and white hawthorn of spring, and smell the lilac and see the rhododendron bush a-bloom. But I always long for England in the autumn, to go crunching through the dry leaves, to turn over the shiny horse-chestnuts, to see the hedgerows covered with berries, and to bring bunches of chrysanthemums in from the misty garden.

This is my first autumn here for twenty years, and I'm enjoying every minute of it. Long ago, before I went to the Middle East, we used to live in the country, but never so near to the woods as my mother lives now, and my little daughter and I go out in search of adventure, and find it in the grey squirrels scampering away up the oak trees and in filling our pockets with more conkers than the boy opposite.

I'm a teacher in Egypt, and I've taught Keats' "Ode to Autumn" over and over again. Can you imagine what it's like never to have seen the leaves turn red and fall? I have to go into elaborate explanations, because in Egypt the leaves don't fall . . . only from one or two trees, and they don't turn hectic red. Maybe the first verse about "mellow fruitfulness" means something to them, because autumn's the time for the date harvest in Egypt, and the palms are weighted down with great heavy clusters of brown and red. It's the season of mists, too, and in the early morning the Nile is heavily shrouded. There are plenty of autumn flowers, but they are not "mournful roses" as Tchekov put it, because Egypt is not dying. This is the time of year when the Nile has flooded and soon the whole valley will be green with the crops of winter. This is the time of the cotton harvest, and when the "white gold", as the Egyptians call it, has been collected, there will be weddings and festivity throughout the countryside. But the days of sitting in the warm sunshine before the open door are over. "Go in and shut the door" say the peasants at this time, for there's money in the house after harvest which must be guarded, and winter days are at hand.

That is the autumn I've known for twenty years; it's beautiful, but it isn't the autumn of stubble-fields, acorns, and bonfires, and somewhere the promise of another spring.

A Litany of Apples

by Jim Holmes

I LOVE HORTICULTURAL shows with their wonderful displays and especially in the apple section—old favourites revive so many happy memories. Ribston Pippin, sweet and nutty, mellow, fragrant, is a joy to eat. Cox's Orange Pippin is first choice these days, and unquestionably one of the best, but discerning palates rate Blenheim Orange just as highly, while many older folk stoutly maintain the old-fashioned russet beats them all. It's a matter of taste and the more variety we have the better; apples, like cheeses and wine, have unique flavours which vary from district to district and year to year. Each has its moment of perfection. The old gardeners, knowing their fruit, only brought them out when at their best, unlike the greedy commercialism of today.

There is romance in our orchards, so much history, so many lucky chance discoveries of seedlings that have found fame. The very names invite a poet's pen. There's Lady Sudeley so sweet and delicate to eat, the Irish Peach, Lady Henniker of curious shape and flavour, Mother's Apple or rather the American Mother so crisp, juicy, and refreshing, a lovely shiny red. Dear old Annie Elizabeth is a splendid long-keeping apple and that old neighbour of mine the Vicar of Beighton of which it is said, "the longer it keeps the better it eats". People who can't resist a bright red apple should try Norfolk Royal, sweet, crisp, juicy, and tasting as good as it looks. Another juicy apple with a distinctive flavour is Allington Pippin, but I especially like Laxton's Superb.

Maybe you are impatient for Cox's Orange? Well try instead the earlier maturing Ellison's Orange and I'm sure you'll like them just as well. For eating later in the year give me the delicious Charles Ross, named after the great gardener who, living from 1825 to 1917, must have seen the introduction of every apple we know today—a wonderful apple and a remarkable man. How about the Sturmers? Finding conditions hard here, they emigrated to Tasmania, made good and now come back to the old country in thousands. On the other hand old Hawthornten, coming south from Scotland, found our climate much to its liking.

What a wonderful choice we have, from Cox to Codlin, from Bramley to Beefing, for eating and for cooking and, of course, for cider.

Nowadays people talk of eating or cooking apples as though there was a dividing line, yet most apples can serve both purposes. The Beauty of Bath, so abused as an eater, is a splendid cooker. Some discerning people even cook Cox's Orange because of its splendid flavour, and the outstanding cooking apple Bramley Seedling makes refreshing eating when fully ripe.

The wonderful Dr. Harvey, so highly esteemed in East Anglia for over 300 years, can truly be said to have stood the test of time. It is a non-acid apple equally good for eating or cooking. This was the traditional mincemeat apple in my native Norfolk, the apple that even today old people lay away for Christmas to bring out as the golden wonder their mothers and grandmothers knew and loved so long ago, when hardly a garden didn't boast its Dr. Harvey tree, the finest physician of them all. Another as good, if not better, is the Majestic Green Queen, a large green apple with a delicate pink flush. It never fails to bear, needs no spraying, keeps until April and bears a crop that has to be seen to be believed! Why the nurserymen neglect this apple beats me. It's near perfection. Do you like baked apples? Try Warners King, one of the biggest baking apples ever seen. Another good eating or cooking apple is Lord Derby, a large ribbed apple. Young housewives who only ask for Cox's or Bramleys don't know what they are missing.

Most of these and many modern varieties I have not mentioned can be seen today, but where are the old-time favourites? Where are the Pearmains, that pear-shaped eating apple renowned for hundreds of years and lingering in old orchards within living memory? We've all heard of the historic Costard apple that costermongers used to sell and after whom they are named. The famous Sapsy Wine, or Saps of wine, whose crimson skin seemed to bleed into its flesh when bitten, a flavour sharper than we like today, is just a tantalizing memory of something precious lost for ever. So many have gone, others linger in private gardens or are only remembered when old-timers bring them back to mind, such as Hales' Wonder, Kirton Pippin, Quarrenden, Boston Russet, King Pippin, Nonpareil, the Norfolk Beefing—a cooking apple famous for generations—and countless russets, pippins and seedlings of purely local fame. D'Arcy Spice I've never seen, but mercifully its qualities were recognized and the old stock saved just in time.

Of course people argue that better varieties have taken their place, but who can be sure? Many russets and pippins so prized when I was a boy are gone for ever. One in particular, a round, flattish small golden russet speckled with white, the sweetest apple I ever knew, can't be found today. Had they been grafted on to modern rootstocks who knows what results we might have seen?

Many districts have apples with unique qualities far too good to lose and not too late to save—and save them we must, they're part of our heritage. If we can save and preserve Puffing Billies and vintage cars surely we can preserve the vintage apples! It's true gardens are changed and few can plant on the grand scale. We'll never see those mighty trees again, the white-washed trunks like ghosts by night, a refuge for so many birds, the storm-cock resting in the highest crotch, the thrushes and chaffinches in the lower limbs, and the smaller garden birds all flitting in and out, a fairyland in spring with song and blossom everywhere. And what a harvest! Long ladders reaching to the sky and still the finest fruit beyond our reach on twiggy tips, a challenge to small boys' athletic limbs. How we dreaded the autumn gales, till all was safely gathered in. And think of all those windfalls carpeting the ground!

Can we save these old varieties? Of course we can. Why not enlist the enthusiasm of young people? If the Education Authorities encourage them to seek out worthwhile survivors, graft them on to suitable root stocks, and plant them around our fine new schools and colleges, what a bond would be established between young and old, what an interest could be added to rural science and horticultural studies! Local tradition would be revived and a living museum created, giving beauty, shade, and harvest, to be enjoyed and remembered all their lives.

Ancient Monuments

by Basil Boothroyd

IF I WERE trying to drive through the middle of Chichester, say, and I got held up by a party of Chinese tourists milling round that fifteenth-century Market Cross there, I should probably be very impatient with them, and just sit there hooting. Which is no way to encourage the tourist trade from Peking.

Actually, I've never had this experience, and between you and me I'm not at all sure how those Chinese got into these remarks. I suppose I was thinking of the traditional Chinese reverence for anything that's very old. And if so it's obvious why I don't share this feeling ... because I haven't a drop of Chinese blood in me and even so, it's a rotten example of the point I'm trying to make, because my father—who was no more Chinese than I am, as far as I know—was an absolutely dedicated, single-minded Ancient Monuments man. He'd go miles out of his way to look at a ruin, or a stone circle, or a lump of Roman pavement. Whenever our summer holidays got to the planning stage it wasn't a matter of deciding between Broadstairs and Westgate-on-Sea so much as between Hadrian's Wall and the megalithic monuments of the Mendips. Sometimes, of course, we got the best of both worlds. I mean, if we settled for King Arthur's Castle at Tintagel, for instance, then at least it was on the Cornish coast, and there was a chance of some bathing and beach cricket and other twentieth-century recreations. All the same, it was quite likely that when Father's turn came to bat, he wouldn't be there. He'd suddenly remembered that there was a very interesting old bit of carved stone near Camelford, and gone wandering off across Bodmin Moor to find it.

Well I suppose by the time I was about twelve we hadn't left a bit of carved stone unturned, between us, and we'd seen so many cathedrals and castles and ruined abbeys and old battlefields and funny tombs and Roman baths and earthworks and long barrows and fascinating epitaphs in ancient cemeteries . . . that of course I could never remember where we'd seen which, or why. And I'm afraid this was a terrible disappointment to him. He never went anywhere without having read six books about it first, so the thing was well lodged in his mind by the time we arrived. But it was just sprung on me. "There we are," he'd say, at the end of another long pilgrimage, "that's Hetty Pegler's Tump." You know, this was something he'd been wanting to see for thirty years, whereas I hadn't. I'd never heard of Hetty Pegler. Never heard of a tump, as a matter of fact. I was just hoping that we should get back to the nearest town before the shops shut, and I could get my copy of the *Magnet*. Mind you, I wouldn't have said so—not only because children's manners were better in those days, but because I was very fond of my Pa, and I liked to see him happy. But I never understood, and I still don't, why he, or anyone else, should be made happy by Hetty Pegler's Tump, or Fingal's Cave, or Offa's Dyke, or the old town pump at Little Walsingham.

It's a curious, but highly enviable gift, this instant response to antiquity, which of course thousands and thousands of people have and I, to my very great regret, have not. If *I* want to get anything out of an antique hunk of masonry, lying in the middle of a field with a chain round it and a notice up from the Ancient Monuments Board saying that it's a bit of a Saxon shrine and penalty five pounds for touching it, I have to work very hard at it before it starts giving off any romantic or archaeological associations. I have to shut my eyes, and tell myself, very slowly and emphatically, "This . . . is . . . a very, very old piece of stone . . . and it's terribly fascinating and marvellous." And so on. And even then, when I open my eyes again and look, it's still very often just this hunk of masonry in the middle of a field with a chain round it. It must just be lack of imagination, I suppose. Because people like my father, gazing on a bit of Saxon shrine, actually see Alfred the Great and Hereward the Wake being chased round it by the Danes and the Normans. It's as good as a Hollywood spectacular to them, so if you're one of them, I do hope you know how lucky you are.

By the way, I'm sorry all those Chinese got in at the beginning, but now I come to think of it, perhaps they have got a bearing on all this after all. Because, surely, it isn't old things they have such a reverence for, but old people—you know, very, very old Chinese Grandmas and Grandpas. The older you get in China, the more you're revered and respected and made a fuss of, whereas in the West we're more inclined to concentrate on getting the old folks out of the way into a nice little Eventide Home. And I go along very much with the Chinese attitude here, I must say. Hetty Pegler's Tump may be a great thrill, but what was ever done, I wonder, for Hetty Pegler, when she got old and frail and too exhausted to make tumps? Nothing, I'll bet. In China she'd have had all the family on the the run with hot bottles and breakfast in bed and the latest library books, begging her to tell them all about the tumps she'd made in her time . . . and otherwise to pour out the wit and wisdom and reminiscences of a long and fascinating life.

I don't say I want to be a Chinese Hetty Pegler. The sex is wrong, for one thing. And I'm not dead yet. But I can see a not-too-distant time when the younger generation rallying round with a footstool and a hot toddy wouldn't come amiss. That's what they do in China. In this country

SOUVENIRS THROUGH THE CENTURIES

Holiday memories are precious but fickle. When people celebrated a holiday yesterday, as today, they sought to retain tangible reminders of their adventures. At the time these usually cost little enough: many a small jug or patch box or scent bottle proclaims itself as a "Trifle" from some once-fashionable resort or watering place. But today they are among our most fascinating small antiques and curios.

Souvenirs of places are often delightful. Many of the finest date to the early 19th century, blue printed in wonderful detail on clear white bone china; others are found in the early Victorian wood mosaic known as Tunbridge ware. But some of the most intriguing souvenirs commemorate public participation in important events. One thinks at once of the glass engraved with Jacobite emblems around the period of the 1745 rebellion or Liverpool delftware painted with the names of Parliamentary candidates. Royalty throughout the 18th and 19th centuries were featured on endless souvenirs, from Bilston transfer-printed enamel snuffboxes bearing marriage portraits of George III and Queen Charlotte, to tough salt-glazed stoneware commiserating with Queen Caroline and including many flat-back chimney ornaments recalling important happenings for Queen Victoria and her family. Early Victorians relished their shrimp paste from Pegwell Bay in pots bearing colour-printed portraits of the Prince Consort and views of Osborne House.

Some of the finest portraits are found among the late 18th-century cameos made by Wedgwood in his fine stonewares and the early 19th-century cameos by Apsley Pellatt enclosed in glass. But there are other souvenirs to be found with little enough to recommend them save a wonderful exuberant liveliness, a sheer delight in living among such world-shattering events as a fight between Humphreys and Mendoza.

Modern souvenirs include mugs and plates commemorating the Silver Jubilee of George V and Queen Mary, Coronations, and such events as The Festival of Britain in 1951 and the World Cup in 1966. Others are bought to remind tourists of their visit to England.

THERLE HUGHES

Canterbury Pilgrims in the 14th century bought souvenirs. The example shown on the previous page depicts St. Thomas of Canterbury. It is four inches high and can be fixed to clothing by means of a pin and clasp.

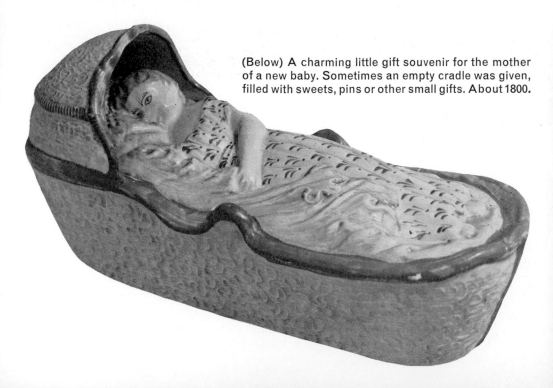

(Below) A charming little gift souvenir for the mother of a new baby. Sometimes an empty cradle was given, filled with sweets, pins or other small gifts. About 1800.

SOUVENIRS OF EVENTS

(Above left) A posset pot commemorating the election of the Mayor and Mayoress of Nottingham in 1700. (Above right) A punch bowl of delftware from Bristol supporting the successful candidates in the Oxfordshire election of 1774. (Left) a lustre-ware ale jug showing the fight between Spring and Langan at Chichester. Sportsmen also kept souvenirs in earthenware of the winners of famous horse and greyhound races and other events.

SEASIDE SOUVENIRS OF BRIGHTON

(Top) A wooden cylinder containing a panoramic view of Brighton sea-front, published by Ackermann in 1833. (Left) A glass paperweight of 1840-50 showing the sea front and Chain Pier. (Above) A wooden work-box illustrated with views of the Royal Pavilion and the Chain Pier, about 1830.

ROYAL SOUVENIRS
(Left) A Doulton brown stoneware figure of Queen Caroline holding a scroll with the words 'My hope is in the People'. (Above) A crystal cameo paperweight depicting Frederick, Duke of York. (Below) A South Staffordshire white-enamelled snuff-box of 1761, commemorating the marriage of George III and Queen Charlotte.

VICTORIAN SOUVENIRS
A pot lid depicting Prince Albert printed in colour. Such lids were first issued in 1846, printed in two colours, but soon more colourful reproductions were on sale. Genuine examples are now keenly collected.

A Staffordshire plate commemorating Queen Victoria's Jubilee in 1887.

ELIZABETHAN SOUVENIRS

Two souvenir mugs designed by Professor Richard Guyatt and made by Wedgwood. (Above) A sporting mug in black jasper decorated with raised white ornamentation in which each letter of the words 'A Souvenir' incorporates famous British sports and sporting events. (Below) A Wedgwood mug commemorating the coronation of Queen Elizabeth II in 1953.

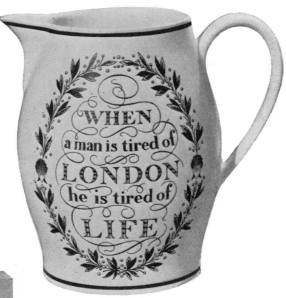

MODERN SOUVENIRS
Three Award Winners in the 1965 British
Souvenirs competition sponsored by the
Council of Industrial Design. The 'Tower of
London' herb jar and the 'London mug' in-
scribed with Dr. Johnson's famous dictum
were produced by Wedgwood. The clock was
made by Image Three Design Associates.

they're all out in fast cars going round the Ancient Monuments, calling at the pubs where Queen Elizabeth slept, seeing Stonehenge by moonlight, or making expeditions to the ancient Stately Homes of England, where the grounds are full of beat groups, shooting galleries and Dukes signing autographs.

I'm not attacking the young—don't think that. But I do have this feeling that perhaps I was young at the wrong time. You never know . . . . if the ancient monuments had been properly managed when I was a lad, with hot dogs for sale at Hadrian's Wall, and Kenilworth Castle full of dodgem cars and candy-floss, and traction-engine rallies in the grounds of Fountains Abbey, I might have taken a more enthusiastic view of the whole business.

WAR YEARS

How Art Thou Translated

by Laurence Cotterell

I WAS A teen-age war poet.

That would have been a splendid title for this article—if only I hadn't been a few years out of my teens at the time. But I was, I suppose, a war poet of sorts, and a young one at that.

One poem of mine which appeared in an Eighth Army anthology got particularly well noticed in the British Press at the time, and picked up some glowing reviews. That statement may seem less than modest, but I think you will see later on that I have a special reason for making it. It began:

> The soul of man once more is on the march;
> The tents of pillowed ease are struck;
> The slow, soft days behind us in the arch
> Of sheltered years amid the ruck.
>
> Hard days, dark nights ahead, no lotus hours
> To sap the muscle of the will
> In cheerful halls, cool rooms and whispered bowers,
> In scented gardens warm and still.

Do we regret our own short, shadowed youth—
That fitful gap 'twixt rage and rage?
Would we have lived in times of golden ruth,
The valley of a peaceful age?

No! We regret not even our own past
Nor envy those who fought no fights.
They never knew our depths, gloom-overcast,
But yet they never knew our heights.

They never stood upon the topmost peak
Where thunder threatens, lightning strikes,
The future's stinging wind upon their cheek,
Before their feet Fate's gleaming spikes.

They never felt within themselves the fire
Of danger and of agony,
To carry forward, upward, ever higher,
The spirit of humanity. . . .

and so it went on in similar vein.

Mr. Siegfried Sassoon wrote a Foreword to this Eighth Army anthology, and he concluded by quoting some lines from my poem as being by a poet who spoke for all the rest. One eminent literary person hailed it as a vivid evocation of Britain at war and democracy on the march.

The fact is we were sitting in our holes in the Libyan desert some time towards the end of 1942, and were thoroughly browned off. We'd been abroad three years already, and there didn't seem much prospect of ever again being anywhere but abroad. Naturally enough the speeches and exhortations of statesmen and politicians had come to have a pretty hollow ring, and when each batch of newspapers reached us from England, we did our best to avoid the dreary, nauseating reports of sickly propaganda blitherings by the Whitehall Warriors and the Westminster Commandos.

Then one day, leafing through a copy of *The Times*, I was struck by a speech which seemed a bit more lively than most. I remember there was a nasty sandstorm raging at the time and intellectual discussion was confined to such problems as whether to make tea and shave in it, or shave first and make tea with the shaving water. Accordingly I sat down in my private hole in the sand and rendered this speech as nearly as possible into verse— into the poem, in fact, from which I have quoted. I was mildly surprised when this piece was selected for inclusion in the Eighth Army anthology of poems by men of the desert forces—and even more surprised when the critics praised it in the terms I have indicated.

Because, you see this was by no means the spirit of Britain at war and democracy on the march. I couldn't say so at the time because officialdom was notoriously short on humour (unless, of course, the jokes were official ones or made ponderously by commanding generals) and I pre- ferred the open desert to a military prison, but the original speech which I had turned into these verses was made by Adolf Hitler to his S.S. divisions. Now turn back and read them again.

There's no moral here. Or perhaps there might be any one of a dozen morals . . . such as wartime propaganda being much the same the world over, or the Devil quoting Holy Writ for his own purpose, or the universality of the sentiments expressed by good men and bad men alike in appealing to their countrymen.

All I know is that if you give me the text of speeches on international relationships by Mr. Harold Wilson, Mr. Edward Heath, Mr. Kosygin, Mr. Lyndon Johnson, Mao Tse-Tung, General De Gaulle and General Franco, I will quickly write you one poem—just one—that will serve as a pretty accurate rendering of any and all of them!

The Black Madonna

*Retold by Robert Rietty from a true story recounted to him by
Graham McRae*

THE TACTICAL HEADQUARTERS of our battalion in the winter line in Italy in December 1944 was at Grizzana. It crouched against its hillside near Monte Salvaro; its houses seeming to climb on each other's shoulders in a vain attempt to peep at the enemy-held territory which was further up over the ridge.

Behind us lay the majestic grimness of Monte Vigese, from where the Black Madonna keeps a friendly eye on the faithful among the people of the village who devoutly believe in her power to invoke miracles. Miracles of healing, mostly, but almost any kind of miracle, providing the supplicant is devoted enough to make the arduous pilgrimage on foot up the steep rough path that leads to her shrine.

Old Mamma Bucciolini, who sometimes did our washing when we went down the line for the periodic rest at Creda, used to tell us tales of crutches cast away, of unbearable grief assuaged, and of childless couples being blessed almost immediately after a visit to the beloved Black Madonna. We used to smile and let her prattle, for faith so child-like and absolute is a lovely thing, not to be ridiculed or decried.

But as Christmas drew nearer there were no pathetic little processions up the mountainside to the shrine, because the bulk of the civilian population had been evacuated, for their safety and for our security. Tales reached us from enemy occupied territory of a different kind of evacuation. Over there, whole families were being "recruited" for labour under the German

Reich, and every day brought fresh stories of boys and girls being dragged off to unknown terrors.

So the trickle of refugees escaping from beyond no-man's-land began to grow until they became a problem in shell-shattered Grizzana—a typical mountain village of steep, narrow streets, and cobbled lanes, where the roof of your neighbour's dwelling is on a level with your front door-step. Most of the buildings had been badly hit and afforded little shelter from the bitter weather, still less from the German guns. All the available cover was crammed with troops—all, that is, except the stable where the officers' mules were kept.

Balanced on the steepest part of the reverse slope on which the village is built, no enemy shell could fall steeply enough to hit that stable; and so all the dejected, exhausted refugees from the German side were kept there until lorries could be spared to ferry them to the camps established for their use near Florence. Interrogating these unhappy people was part of my job, and the information thus garnered enabled us to build up a picture of the German line in the serried, snow-blanketed ranges between us and Bologna.

On the morning of December 24, I went down the village street to see the R.S.M. about wangling some extra Christmas cheer for the members of my section. War or no war, we were going to celebrate, and the N.A.A.F.I. had laid on the means for anyone who could pay for it. We held our party in the cellar of the Headquarters building that night. The line was fairly quiet, but one of our fighting-patrols made contact early on and captured a dozen prisoners. We identified them as belonging to the 274th Grenadier Regiment of the Wehrmacht, put them under guard in the mule stable, and returned to our celebrating.

It was a good party—a very good party. As far as I can remember, it must have been half past ten when we broke it up and rolled into our blankets. At eleven o'clock an orderly called me to go down to the stables to interrogate a batch of Italian civilians who wanted to give information; no one else could understand them.

My head ached and the icy wind bit through my great-coat as I stumbled over the cobbles and as I wormed my way through the black-out curtains on the stable-door I hit my head on the lintel. The stable was empty of its rightful occupants who had gone off on their nightly errand, carrying supplies to the forward positions. A hurricane lantern guttered in the corner where the German prisoners huddled in their straw. Between them and the door was the most pathetic tableau I have ever seen.

An emaciated young man, obviously an advanced tuberculosis case, was coughing up bright red blood and spitting it into little wads of straw. A silver-haired ancient sat giggling and grimacing at the Germans, his high cackle horrible to hear, utter vacancy in his eyes. Five children between the ages of four and nine lay in a deep sleep of complete exhaustion round a young girl, her head draped in a shawl, an old army blanket falling loosely about her. She sat upright but at her ease, busy binding the torn foot of the smallest child, She was not particularly beautiful but the compassion in her eyes and on her mouth gave my heart a twist.

Behind her, and dominating the group, stood the matriarch. White haired and deeply tanned, aquiline of feature and proud of bearing, she spoke quietly to the imbecile and he fell silent immediately.

Turning to me, she said that she had information to impart, perhaps valuable, perhaps not, depending on whether others who had come before her had spoken truly. She then gave me a most detailed word picture of the disposition of the enemy's artillery, apparent strength on the ground, and so on. The German prisoners muttered indignantly, but her measured tones never faltered.

I made precise notes of all she told me, stopping now and again to question her closely on some particular point, letting the Germans mutter angrily, for their reaction showed her testimony to be true. Eventually she seemed to grow impatient, as if she must hurry through this business to be ready for something more important.

At last I got annoyed.

"What's your hurry?" I asked.

She pointed to the girl. "Signore," she said, "her time is very near. Last month they took her father, who is my son. Last night they took her husband. He fought, so they killed him before her eyes. She too wished to die, to let his child within her die with her. I bethought me of the Madonna Nera, and I prayed—and then I knew that I must leave our village and come to the shrine of the Madonna by the shortest road, for she would intercede, and the good God would guide us to safety.

"And so your soldiers brought us here, and I brought these helpless ones too, for I had nowhere to leave them and without me they cannot fend."

"I see," I said. "Tell me, how long before . . . before the girl . . ."

"Within the hour, Signore."

I admit it, I panicked. I shouted to the sentry to send one of the guard for the Medical Officer, and started to fuss about where we could put the girl, whose face was now drawn with pain, her finger nails digging into her palms.

But the old lady smiled. "Signore, Signore!" she reproved me gently. "There is no cause for alarm. Another homeless one, long ago, bore her child in a manger—and see, are there not mangers here?"

So between us we laid the girl in a manger. I turned away, and made the prisoners turn their faces to the wall. It was an amazingly quick and easy birth, yet it seemed hours before the child's thin wail broke the silence. I looked at my watch. Exactly one minute past midnight—Christmas morning.

Not long afterwards I heard a scuffling at the door and went to investigate. Outside in the bitter cold were two or three men from the company in reserve. One of them sidled in.

"Look, Sarge," he whispered, "the blokes heard about this kid an' . . . an' all that—so we passed the hat round—an' well . . . well here's a box of doings, an' some grub!" And he hurried off into the night.

There was just about everything in that box—talcum powder, toilet paper, sweets, soap, a mouth organ, mufflers, pullovers, tooth-paste. . . .

As I carried the gifts to the matriarch, the sentry called out:

"Just a mo', Sarge! One of these types is being a nuisance. Says he's got to speak to you."

"Send him across," I called back, and a young German marched across the floor and halted smartly in front of me.

"If this young devil wants trouble he can have it!" I thought to myself. "Arrogant brute!"

But he wasn't arrogant. He held out a thin gold cross on a fine gold chain. "If it is permitted," he said, "we have bought it from Heinrich here for the little one. We have given him all we have. Heinrich's share will be the money we still owe him. It has been in his family for many years. May we give it to the mother?"

Remembering what the girl had suffered at the hands of men wearing German uniforms, I hesitated. But the old lady spoke quietly from her station by the manger.

"Wise men came bearing gifts into a stable. Have you forgotten? There is a wisdom beyond wars and all men's folly. . . ."

She took him by the arm and led the prisoner to the girl's side. She spoke gently, but insistently. The mother looked away, white-faced, lips compressed. For a long, long moment she stayed like that, then turned and reached out a thin hand. And as she took the gift for her son between her fingers, she looked into the prisoner's eyes, and smiled.

As I left the stable to go back and write out my report, the haunting strains of *Stille Nacht* came softly from the prisoners' corner. I was tempted to go back to the stores and wangle a bottle to split with all the people inside—prisoners of war and all—but I decided I had better not.

So I didn't. And that is one of my deepest regrets.

Caucasian and U.39

by Admiral Sir William Jameson

AT 5.45 A.M. on the first of July 1915 the small tanker *Caucasian*, was outward bound in ballast from London to Norfolk, Virginia. It was a perfect summer morning. The sun was shining, there was no wind, and *Caucasian*, about eighty miles south of the Lizard, rustled slowly westward across a calm sea. All round the horizon was sharp and clear; no other ship was in sight. But *Caucasian* was keeping a sharp look-out. U-boats had been active off Land's End and she felt very much alone.

Suddenly a U-boat appeared, approaching on the surface at high speed and flashing a signal. To conserve their limited supply of torpedoes U-boats would order merchant ships to stop, tell their crews to abandon ship, and sink them by gunfire or with demolition charges. Now *Caucasian* had no gun. Her maximum of nine knots was less than that of the U-boat. There was every excuse for her master, Captain F. H. Robinson, to comply with the order to "abandon ship at once". But such action doesn't seem even to have entered his head. He told his Chief Engineer to produce the maximum power the tanker's old engine was capable of and made off, steering a zig-zag course to hinder the aim of the submarine's gun, which had immediately opened fire.

For over an hour the chase went on. The submarine's gun was a small one and she was too far off to fire a torpedo. Several shells hit the *Caucasian* without doing vital damage. Some passed through the top of the bridge where Captain Robinson was standing, watching the U-boat slowly closing in, and this was too much for the steersman in the wheelhouse below who abandoned his post. Leaving the second mate to report the

U-boat's progress Captain Robinson took the wheel himself. Then as the submarine gained ground her gunfire became more accurate. But sixteen hits on the hapless *Caucasian* failed to stop her. The seventeenth crashed into the bridge structure close to the Captain and wrecked the compass and steering standard. The tanker was now unmanageable. She circled to a stop and her crew began to lower the boats. Captain Robinson, who had miraculously escaped injury, looked round for his dog, tucked the terrified animal under his arm and followed his crew.

The submarine was now lying close by with her gun trained on the open boats. It was *U.39*, one of the latest German boats, and commanded by a Lieutenant-Commander Walter Forstmann. Forstmann was understandably angry. The *Caucasian* had given him a long chase and caused him to expend a great deal of ammunition. He shouted across the water that as the Captain had ignored his order to stop and abandon ship, he intended to sink the boats.

The tanker's crew crouched down waiting for death. Then suddenly there came a curious distraction. The Captain's dog fell overboard and Robinson promptly jumped in to rescue it. The dog swam towards the U-boat and was trying to clamber up its steep and slippery side when Captain Robinson caught it up. With its master's arm around it the dog ceased to struggle. Close above them the faces of the Germans looked down at the elderly man with his wet, but trusting dog, gently rising and falling in the swell. A few yards off lay the boats with the rest of the tanker's crew, helpless, silent, and tense with shock.

Lieutenant-Commander Forstmann's anger slowly seeped away; he was baffled. War to him was a serious business, to be ruthlessly pursued. A few moments before he wouldn't have hesitated to carry out his threat and shell the boats. The men in them were, to him, impersonal, "the enemy", but the old man clinging to his submarine with a dog under his arm was a fellow human being. He just couldn't murder him in cold blood.

"You jump overboard to save a dog!" he growled. Captain Robinson stared up at him and made no reply. Except for the swirl of the water against the sides of the submarine it was very quiet. Both Germans and British waited for the next move.

"Go away," Forstmann said impatiently. "Your boats may proceed."

This is no fairy story. The facts are recorded in a stilted official report, laboriously written by a man more at home with a marline-spike than a pen, which Captain Robinson made on his safe return to land. It's among the Board of Trade papers in the Public Record Office for anyone to read for himself.

Here Is Home

by Janet Hitchman

THE MANAGEMENT HAD tacked Birmingham on to the end of the tour. Birmingham! Reputedly the worst place in England for theatrical lodgings. I was suspicious as soon as Ted, the stage carpenter, gave me the address; for no "pro" ever divulges a really good address, more so when I found he wasn't going there himself, but at this late date, I had no option but to take it. "Nice old gal," Ted had said, "that is if you don't mind Jews," adding as an afterthought, "and a bit of row."

Finally after a long, slow war-time journey I stood on the step of a dingy house in a dingy street, miles it seemed from the theatre, listening to the bit of row coming from within. It was compounded of hammering, laughter, full-blast wireless and a female voice in a foreign language.

During a slight lull, I took the opportunity of crashing on the door with the knocker.

Another female voice yelled from the upper regions, "Daivid-d, wotcher think you're doing of? Go and open the doo-er."

The hammering stopped, the wireless was caught and tamed, and a small boy opened the door. He was followed by an enormous woman who seemed to fill the passage, the prototype of all Jewish mommas.

"You come!" she screamed like one from a besieged city welcoming the relief. "The journey was terrible, yes. The bombs, the guns, the dirt. Peoples all shoving like cattle yes—I know. Is terrible to travel. All my people tell me every week."

Actually apart from its slowness the journey hadn't been too bad, and our company had travelled in reserved compartments, but she was so enjoying the horrors I ought to have endured I didn't like to disillusion her.

"Never mind. Here is home. Come and see Poppa and eat."

I followed her into the living-room-cum-kitchen. It was of the usual size found in workers' terrace-houses run up at the end of last century. At that moment it contained besides momma and myself—Poppa sitting in an armchair by the fire, David in the corner making something with wood, Miriam, the daughter, who had just come down from the bed-room—and five Chinese gentlemen.

Momma introduced us, "Is acrobats, Cheng-Tu brothers. Have no English." She indicated each of the five in turn, who smiled and bowed at the wave of her hand. "Is not really brothers; is oncle; is nephew; is nephew; is cousin; is friend of oncle." "Friend of oncle" giggled and looked coy. Momma lowered her voice to a whisper that could have reached no further than the end of the street. "Is probably woo-man."

It is still a mystery to me how she sorted out their relationships.

At that time I was a vegetarian and had mentioned this when I booked the room. I reminded Momma of this as she began dishing out soused herrings.

"You see, I don't eat meat or——"

"I know, I know, you are humanitarian. I have had humanitarians before. Will not kill the animals, I know. For you especially, I stand in queue for the herrings." And so saying she plonked one before me.

The situation was extremely awkward—for just at this time we were beginning to learn the full horror of the Jewish persecutions in Germany; and we were all feeling guilty and sensitive towards the Jews. If I refused to eat the unvegetarian herring, would this not be one more insult to Momma's race? Would she and Poppa, Miriam and David be one fraction more persecuted? I ate that herring, and his brothers every night for a week.

"Are you on the bill with the Cheng-tus?" asked Miriam.

"Oh goodness no; they're in variety. I'm in the legitimate theatre," I replied, with the usual arrogance assumed by the "straight" player.

Momma again waved her hand towards the Chinese, who smiled and bowed into their plates, "And these is bastards—yes?"

I was to find my sensitivity about Hitler's persecutions wasted on Momma. She had known it all many years before when she and Poppa had fled from Lithuania during the Czarist pogroms.

"We come to England, me and Poppa. We have only the Menorah wrapped in rags. I speak no English—Poppa speak no English. Is so funny!" She roared with laughter and Poppa was convulsed by a silent storm of gaiety. It must have been strangely funny; to be young, penniless and virtually speechless in an alien land, with only the Chanukah candle-stick to light the way.

I looked towards the Menorah gleaming on the sideboard. The shape was a miracle of simplicity but it was nickel-plated.

"You brought *that* from Lithuania forty years ago?"

"Yes, we wrap it up—we pretend it was baby. We were bad to say such thing—Poppa and me only engaged, not married."

"They had burned the synagogue you see. So we come here to England," said Poppa—making it sound like a trip to Margate. Momma could see I was puzzled by the Menorah. "Was brass—Miriam's young man works at the plating—he dip it for us." I must have betrayed a shade of horror for she went on defensively, "Now—most beautiful Menorah is in all Boiming-gam."

I had fully intended after the first day to try for better digs nearer the theatre, but in spite of the herring and the Five Cheng-tus doing acrobatics in the room above my head, I couldn't hurt Momma's feelings by going, and after all it was only for a week. The drama that surrounded her was so much more enthralling than the drawing-room comedy I was managing at the theatre. I became as anxious as she to solve the riddle of "friend of oncle" and then there were the preparations for David's Bar-Mitzvah.

"Is ceremony," explained Momma, "for when he is twelve. He reads the Scrolls in the synagogue, and he answers the Rabbi's questions. For all Jewish boys it is so. It has always been so."

"Then we have a party," shouted David "—and I make a speech, and we eat, and I get presents—then I shall be a *man*."

"Ho, ho, ho, you hear that Poppa? Our Daivid will be a man." Momma aimed a swipe at Poppa's shoulders, which if he hadn't, no doubt after years of practice, dodged, would have knocked him senseless.

Oncle and "friend of oncle" came in—almost, but not quite, holding hands. After various nods and giggles, gestures and bows, Momma announced to Miriam, "They won't be in for tea—they have a rehearsal."

"All of them?"

After another graphic discussion the Chinese departed and Momma said, "All but the cousin."

I could not help thinking how wasted Momma was in Birmingham— she should have been an ambassador-at-large.

I said something like that to her.

"But here is home, I could not leave Boiming-gam. For forty years Poppa and me, we live in this house, we have not been out of Boiming-gam since we left Lithuania. Have we, Poppa?"

"Is a long time, but not too long to live in so beautiful a place," said Poppa. "David my son will have a happy Bar-Mitzvah."

"I will have a bang-on super Bar-Mitzvah."

They all agreed he would have a wonderful entry into manhood, and they gazed at him with such love, one could almost feel its wings enfolding him. Here I thought is the secret of the Jews—this indestructible family love.

"Not like my Bar-Mitzvah," said Poppa. "We had to go into a cellar, and I had to read the word and give the answers in whispers. There was no party—no present—only a little thing my sister found in the street— she gave it to me for a lucky Bar-Mitzvah. You know what it was?"

He took his watch-chain from his pocket, and there was a small lead crucifix.

"You see—your Jesus. I have kept it ever since. But for David it will be different, here in this beautiful Boiming-gam."

So the noisy, gay week passed, and Momma came to the door to see me off. We watched oncle and "friend of oncle" walk arm in arm down the street. "Poppa says is not woo-man. Is some other thing," she hissed. "But is nice peoples. All my peoples is nice peoples. Never do the flitting or make complaints."

"Sholom," I said; I had learnt it from a play. Momma was transported. "Sholom! Poppa, she say Sholom. Daivid-d, come and say Sholom— Miriam, she say Sholom."

They all came into the hall, delighted with me, and full of wonder that I, a gentile, should know one of their words.

"You will come again," roared Momma. "When you come to Boiming-gam, you come again." With a wide open gesture, she took in the whole great city, "Here is home."

The Last Train from Prague

by Trude Dub

ON THE 15TH of March 1939, I woke up from an uneasy sleep and switched on my bedside radio. The time was 5.30 in the morning. The place was Prague.

The voice of the announcer said:

"Please keep law and order—the German army is invading Czechoslovakia from all four sides. . . . Please keep law and order—the German army is invading Czechoslovakia from all four sides. . . . Please keep law and order. . . ."

I woke my husband and together we listened to the voice that proclaimed not only the death of one of the finest democracies in Europe, but also the end of an epoch in our lives—an epoch that meant roots, security and human dignity. Even as that voice droned on, we were being turned into fugitives—our crime being that we were Jews.

By about midday, the first convoy of German tanks entered Wenceslas Square. I had often stood there, watching processions in the colourful Czech and Slovak national costumes and cheering with the onlookers. But the crowd that lined both sides of the Square as the first German tank rolled down this beautiful thoroughfare, was as still and silent as the statue of St. Wenceslas, the patron Saint of Bohemia, towering above the Square.

And the Germans did not waste much time. A curfew was called immediately and their lorries rumbled late into the night collecting the first blacklisted victims. In the days that followed, my husband and I ran from embassy to embassy, trying to find a way of escape. By one of those

196

strange coincidences that shape human destinies, we met an old friend, who told us that until the end of March Czech nationals did not require a visa for England. We made up our minds on the spot, although it seemed impossible to get all the necessary documents in the remaining eight days. We did not even have a passport. Never will I forget that breathless paper-chase, the hours in endless queues, with hope mounting and hope disappearing whilst time was running out.

God only knows how we managed it all—the passport, the practically unobtainable railway tickets, the inland revenue permit, the release from the army and lastly, the most difficult thing of all, the Gestapo permit to leave.

There was a possibility of my husband being arrested, so I decided to go to the Gestapo alone. When I came out of that building, I knew that I should never be afraid as long as I lived. I spent the fear of a lifetime in there.

The passports had to be left behind and were to be collected with the permits, if any, three days later, on the day when the last train was leaving Prague to reach England without a visa.

Early that morning, my husband Izio and I set out for the Gestapo. We closed the door of our home on all the precious things we had collected in our young married life, as well as on our hopes and dreams for the future.

We joined the long, long queue. Friends brought us food, whilst the family waited at the flat for our telephone call to bring our luggage to the station. The hours passed and we made only little progress. My God, shall we never reach the door? Round about midday we were getting within sight, but then the officials called a break and the queue became once more motionless.

Two o'clock came and the door opened again. We were not very far from the entrance by this time, but to our dismay the jackbooted Nazi in charge started to pull out his friends from the back of the queue. At 3 p.m. I plucked up all my courage and pointed out, most humbly and politely, that our train would be leaving just after four o'clock. The man yelled:

"Keep your mouth shut, Jewish swine, or you'll go to the back of the queue."

More waiting. . . . At 4 p.m. we were at last moving through the door. A woman in front of us undertook to ring my parents and ask them to bring our hurriedly packed personal belongings to the station.

We arrived at the station within minutes of the train's departure—perhaps it was better so—there was no time for prolonged goodbyes. . . .

The train moved slowly out and I saw the dear faces of my parents disappearing in the distance. I never saw them again.

None of us three hundred fugitives on that train knew that the husbands who were going out to prepare the ground for their wives and children, would never be joined by them, nor were the separated sweethearts to meet again. . . .

Now we were on our way into the unknown. What would happen if England refused us entry? Our speculations were cut short by an order to change trains. This was to be a direct train from Prague to the Dutch port of Vlissingen but Jews were not supposed to ask questions.

We had to change twice more and so precious hours were lost. It now became obvious that we should not reach England before midnight on March 31.

Full of foreboding, the transport reached Bentheim, on the German-Dutch border. There we were told that England would not let us in. It was too late. The treaty would expire before we could reach the English shore.

Now the Dutch also refused us entry, fearing that we would be left on their hands. Besides, their reception centres for refugees in transit were already overcrowded. Negotiations with the Dutch authorities were set afoot, whilst we had to submit ourselves to German customs and police examination. After that we were interned on the train.

Like men in a doomed submarine we sat and waited for three days and nights. What was to become of us? The German railways demanded the use of the train but we could not go forward and we could not go back. We were trapped. Rumours reached us that we might be transferred to a concentration camp.

But now the world was told of our plight by desperate telephone and telegraph messages, and on the fourth day a British Immigration Officer arrived in Oldenzaal—on the Dutch side of the border—to interview and grant visas to suitable subjects.

Izio and I had a chance meeting with an Englishman in Prague on the very day Hitler marched in. Clutching at straws we wired him—and he sent us a guarantee to Oldenzaal. It was only one railway station away but what a different world awaited us on the other side of the border. The Dutch went all out to welcome us and I shall never forget the warmth of their hospitality. Fortified by food and the guarantee of our English friend, we faced the Immigration Officer with easy hearts.

We got the visa and were taken to Hengelo, one more railway stop down the line, to spend the night. As at Oldenzaal, the whole town turned out to greet us. People threw their homes open to us and Scouts took care of our luggage and shepherded us to our lodgings. Izio and I followed our Boy Scout as in a dream through the darkening streets of Hengelo. The crisis was over—this was the beginning of a new life.

That night, after what seemed like a lifetime, we rested again on clean and comfortable beds. Next morning, our group left Hengelo to the chorus of "Long Live Holland" and "Long Live Czechoslovakia". The Boy Scouts formed a guard of honour at the station. I have often thought of this scene, when, a few months later, Holland herself became the victim of the same cruel oppressor.

The journey on the boat was uneventful. We felt that whatever lay before us could never be as bad as our first glimpse of Hitler's rule. True, we did not know a word of English; we had exactly sixpence left after sending postcards from the boat and treating ourselves to one cup of coffee between the two of us; we did not know a soul in England, apart from that chance acquaintance of ours, but we were young and not afraid of hard work. And so, on the first night of Passover—when Jewish people all over the world celebrate their deliverance from slavery to freedom—we landed on these blessed shores.

A CHRISTMAS HAMPER

"Santa Claus—Sheffield"

by Bill Taylor

CHRISTMAS AT ANY age is important, but when you're climbing up to six and it's your first Christmas since you started school, then it becomes kind of special—at least, that's what I believe.

For weeks on end I remember being completely under the spell of an old gentleman with long white whiskers and a red cloak. I wrote umpteen letters in red crayon on blue sugar-bag paper and popped them into the pillar-box, addressed to: SANTA CLAUS, SHEFFIELD. . . .

Once I caught the postman reading one of my lists. "Ummm! tha'll be lucky," he said, which remark was very encouraging, coming as it did from one of His Majesty's Postmen!

Older children at school told me there was no such person as Santa Claus, but I just didn't wish to know that. I boasted about all the things he was going to bring me: a carpentry set, a tram conductor's outfit, a panorama, and a diabolo. Another time it was to be a clockwork train with rails and a tunnel, and a magic lantern with lots and lots of slides.

My mother wisely cautioned me not to "count my chickens". "If tha doesn't stop worritin'," she said, "he waint cum at all. He knows wheer tha lives, tha knows." Yes, he knew where I lived—that was a comforting thought. In fact, everybody knew where I lived. I was the little lad at the fish 'n' chip shop.

Then, something happened to spoil it all. The joyous, colourful landscape of my imagination vanished. Gone was the glittering snow, the tall candlelit trees, the prancing reindeer, and the sleigh. Gone too, was Santa Claus. A simple postcard had changed all that.

It was a card from my Aunty Flo at Dobbin Hill to say she wouldn't be spending Christmas with us as planned. It wasn't that that upset me, but the suggestion that we should spend our Christmas at Dobbin Hill.

Mind you, at any other time I'd have been glad to go there for a holiday. But, well, this Christmas was rather special—I mean, my going to school and all that. Besides, Mother had reminded me often enough that Santa Claus knew where I lived; but, I reasoned, he wouldn't expect to find me at Dobbin Hill.

The day for our departure arrived. I sat with a scowl on my face all the way in the tram. When we got there Aunty Flo said I looked "reight badly". "What ails the lad?" she inquired. "Nowt," my mother replied. "He's a damn seet better in health than temper."

True, the cottage looked real Christmassy, what with the blazing fire, the light from the oil lamps and holly and evergreens stuck in the picture frames, and on the dresser was a real Christmas tree in a pink plant-pot.

I perked up a bit when I saw there were potatoes baked in their jackets for tea. At the mention of bed-time, though, I was down-in-the-dumps again. Still, I hung up one of Mother's black stockings as usual, but without any enthusiasm. "Fat lot of good that'll be," I muttered peevishly.

I must have cried myself to sleep. Something woke me—perhaps the moonlight slanting across my face, or maybe it was the carollers singing further down the lane.

I lay there for a few moments, and though my eyes were still drowsy with sleep, I could see the stocking on the bed-rail was looking limp and dejected.

Suddenly I became wide awake. I slipped from the bed and crossed the cold oilcloth to the latticed window. Snow was falling. It was settling on

Aunty Flo's raggy little garden, all moist and glistening like soapsuds on a washday. A lamp was burning in a window of the farmhouse where Aunty bought her butter, milk and eggs.

Then I saw it! A pony and cart had stopped outside Aunty Flo's gate, and, coming up the garden path, through the swirling snowflakes, was an old man. Over his shoulder he carried a sack. "I've seen him—he's found me." With my heart nigh bursting I climbed into bed, resolved not to go to sleep. . . .

Yet somehow I missed him. It was morning before I saw the long black stocking, bulging, irregular, and excitingly grotesque!

Later, when all the Merry Christmasses had been said, and I'd examined the contents of the stocking over and over again, down to the apple and orange and the three new pennies in the toe, I overheard Aunty say to Mother:

"Ee! owd Sammy wa' latish comin' wit' firewood last neet. I thowt happen he'd forgotten me."

"Sammy? No, no," I blurted in my anguish. I saw the scurrying snowflakes, the pony and cart, and the old old man with the sack. His name trembled on my tongue, then slid safely back inside me, to become a childhood memory.

About two years later, just before Christmas I got a seasonal job and another memory. It happened like this. Chalked on a slate hanging on the door jamb of *"Timm. High Class Butcher. Families waited on daily"* were the words: LAD WANTED. NIGHTS AND SATURDAYS. APPLY WITHIN.

That evening, on my mother's instructions, I applied.

Though she had urged me to "mek haste", I walked at a snail's pace, hoping to arrive too late—but apparently a snail's pace was too quick for the slate was still there, and I don't mind admitting I was crestfallen.

To me, Mr. Timm really looked like a butcher. I mean, even without the blue-striped apron, the white jacket, and the sharpening-steel dangling from his waist, no one could have mistaken him for a fishmonger, a barber, or a muffin man.

"Can tha carry a fore-quarter on thi shoulder?" he asked me.

"Noaw, sir," I answered brightly, thinking I should certainly be turned down.

"No," he said, contemplating me gravely and pushing his straw ben further back on his head, "I don't think tha could." And then, as if deciding to make the best of a bad job, he said, "Aye, tha'll do. Start tomorrow at five sharp!"

I was about eight years old then, and there were nights when I'd rather have played tiggy with the lads; but I soon began to enjoy my work as an errand boy. Every night after school I gulped down a mug of tea, rammed down some bread and dripping, and set off to work with a clean, white apron under my arm.

The customers' orders were laid out on the slab at the end of the shop. Here, among the choicest English cuts, were fine York hams, Aylesbury ducks, and crusty, golden-brown pork pies, not to mention Mrs. Timm's home-made souse and potted meats.

When the orders were ready I lunged through the shop, my basket crammed full and bumping against my bony hip and the sawdust on the shop floor creeping through the eyelets of my laced-up boots.

Occasionally a kindly disposed customer rewarded me with a penny. More often than not I'd buy a comic, and perching myself on the edge of the basket I'd soon become engrossed in the adventures of "Weary Willie and Tired Tim", or in the latest crazy antics at "Casey's Court". This, I'm afraid was rather detrimental to Timm's delivery service. . . .

"I'm havin' no more of this, mi lad!" an exasperated cook-general would say. "I've a good mind ter send it back!" or "This meat ought to have been int' oven twenty minutes ago—it's same every blessed time I've cump'ny ter cook for."

But with typical Yorkshire generosity they often gave me a newly baked tea-cake or a kissing crust. " 'Ere's summat ter keep the worms from nibblin'," they'd say, "though, bless me, tha' dusn't deserve it."

Then it was almost Christmas. . . . The gas mantles in the shop were new and bright with glossy green holly hanging from the brackets. Even

Mr. Timm looked Christmassy with a tantalizing sprig of mistletoe in the ribbon of his straw hat. And in the window was a fine Boar's Head, beautifully decorated and bearing a coloured card with the words:

WISHING ALL OUR CUSTOMERS THE COMPLIMENTS OF THE SEASON

. . . and high on the runner-rails were rows and rows of prime turkeys, each with a gay rosette pinned to its breast.

On my rounds I saw Christmas trees ablaze with dancing firelight trapped in baubles of coloured glass; and snow, as white as white, riding high on the tram trolleys. And everywhere there were rosy-cheeked apples, and tangerines, and rich fruit cakes dressed in petticoats of frilled paper, and boxes and boxes of red and green crackers sparkling with silver frost.

At last it was Christmas Eve, with the sound of carols and the promise of Christmas Day—full stockings, warm mince pies, and the exciting blue flames licking huge plum puddings boiled as dark and round as bowlers' woods. . . .

When the last order had been delivered and the empty baskets well and truly scrubbed, I wished Mr. Timm "Good neet and a Merry Christmas" and made my way home carrying a parcel and my wages. I mention the parcel first because the three shillings I'd earned, though a princely sum in those days, was as nothing compared to the pleasure to be seen on my mother's face when she saw the treasures I had brought.

"Now isn't that grand!" she exclaimed as she surveyed the sausages, the scrag-end, and the nice bit of pie-meat the parcel contained. I showered on her lots of gleaming new pennies—tips from that wonderful Christmas at Timm's. Then, as a thought struck her, she said, "Ee, son, I hope you remembered yer manners!"

Though it was well past my bed-time she let me have my fort and wooden soldiers out on the hearth-rug for half an hour, though long before the time was up I must have fallen asleep, for I never remembered being undressed and carried upstairs to bed. . . .

Eat, Drink And Be Moody

by Basil Boothroyd

I'D JUST LIKE to say, first of all, that if my wife's listening she needn't bother, because she knows all this. All right, darling? You just put your feet up with a good cookery-book—or cook-book, as they call them nowadays—"cuk-buk", it sounds like some sort of ailment you catch in Swaziland. Still, never mind. No, it's marvellous, really, that our marriage has survived all this time, because it's always had this one hopeless incompatibility—my wife loves cooking and I hate food. If I'd married anyone a bit more litigation-prone she'd have sued me for mental cruelty years ago. I don't know how she'd have got on. I mean, if things had been the other way about, me loving food and her hating cooking. *I* could probably have sued *her* with great success. It's a wife's responsibility to provide her husband with food, I suppose. But would any Judge say that it's the husband's responsibility to eat it? I don't know. You'd probably have to have demonstrations in the Court, with Fanny and Johnny Cradock subpœnaed as expert witnesses.

However, let's get down to the facts. I don't actually hate food. That's an exaggeration. If I'm really hungry I'll have a plate of soup or a small boiled egg with the next man. But not both. It's when you've had the soup, and feel ready to get back to work with only five minutes wasted, that they come fussing round with some enormous fish or other, and expect you to have that. And if as a matter of courtesy you manage to force some of it down, they're back again in two shakes with a lot of meat and gravy, and whole flotillas of vegetable dishes floating down the table, even things like parsnips, sometimes—or do I mean artichokes, they've got a sort of smoky taste, like old fireplaces—and very often several sorts of potato. I mean, supposing one wants potatoes at all, who wants several sorts of potato? It's just meaningless duplication. You might just as well go about with two shirts on. And then, after all that, there's the dreaded moment when you're staggering up from the table, wondering what on earth an X-ray photograph of your inside would look like just then, when they come in with an apple charlotte and custard, and probably a lot of cheese lined up ready to strike the final deadly blow.

Now, I've had people to dine in my house—because I have to let my wife have one of these wild cooking binges from time to time, just as a sort of therapy, you know—and they seem to have nothing but praise and admiration for this sort of performance. As the great dishes and tureens and hot-plates and things come steaming along, their eyes light up and they all have second helpings, and the wives say, "What *have* you put in this delicious sauce?" and it turns out to be something they'd absolutely never have thought of, like grated passion-fruit pips or a tablespoonful of cold tea, and everyone's amazed—and the husbands say to me afterwards, "By jove, old man, you're lucky, having a cook like that on the strength. Never tasted such devilled turbot"—or whatever it was. I never knew what it was, anyway: thought it was some sort of fritter.

Of course, the war made all this a lot worse for me. Before the war, if you remember, it wasn't at all the done thing to *talk* about food. Your hostess did her nut with bouillabaisse and stuffed truffles and pigs' trotters in sauerkraut and all that, and you just sat there stuffing it down and talking about how Mussolini had improved the Italian railways. It was rotten for the hostess, but much better for me. I mean eating's bad enough: having to talk about it's awful. But then of course when rationing came in this ancient and honourable tradition was abandoned; anyone who turned up with half an ounce of butter in an old cold-cream pot set the key of the conversation for the whole evening. And after the meal, such as it was, everyone was exchanging addresses where you could get black-market

o

fish-paste or rabbit pieces. And so this new convention was born, and nowadays, as well as cooking food and eating food, everybody's reading about food and talking about food, and spending all weekend over those illustrated colour supplements full of great rainbow photographs of steak and kidney puddings and hot chocolate sauce being poured on red, green and heliotrope ice cream sundaes.

Now if I wanted a picture of food, which I don't, but, I mean, if I had to have one—you know, as a punishment, or something—I'd try to settle for a small rissole plumb in the middle of a large plate. After looking at that for about three days it's just possible I might feel the old taste-buds uncurling. But if I'd fasted for a fortnight and you showed me one of those loaded plates with the steak actually hanging over the edges, it'd only make me go another month with nothing but an occasional plain biscuit.

I don't defend this, and I can't explain it. I'm perfectly healthy. "You'll faint in the street," people often say to me, when they've eaten a nine-course meal with me and I've settled for some celery fronds and a bit of lightly-done dry toast. But I never have. The only time I shall faint in the street will be after a nine-course meal, and it'll be a judgement on whoever stood over me and made me eat it.

I haven't left much time for drink, but it takes less time than food, and it's another rather unfortunate thing with me that I don't need much drink either, anyway, less than a lot of people do. I know men who take a large Scotch on each quarter-hour from opening time to "Drink Up Gentlemen Please!" and they could still say "Six Czech cricket critics" fifteen times without muffing it. I'm entirely different. Any house I go to and they give me more than one drink an hour, I'm in and out of the sitting room wearing all their hats and singing. It's an economy, in a way, I suppose, but it can get you a terrible name as a party wrecker—while the other chaps, whose back teeth are permanently floating, get asked everywhere. I don't know.

The thing is, I just want you to think of me at Christmas. It's a very bad time for me. One year I was lucky. The goose caught fire and was burnt out, so I was let off with a couple of chipolatas, a slice of orange and a mince pie. But you can't hope for that to happen with any regularity. So there I shall be on Christmas Day, just like you, surrounded with good things—which I just happen to regard as bad things—and my wife, in this rather *split* sort of capacity, trying to get the turkey and cranberry sauce into me with one hand, and keeping me away from the bottles with the other. I can see her point. It must be awful when she's been four hours in the kitchen cooking a meal I didn't eat, and now she is washing it up and all I'm doing to help is stand there singing and wearing the guests' hats.

But anyway—*you* have a Happy Christmas. Don't worry about me. I shall get through, somehow.

Singing "Messiah"

by Keith Parry

I WAS BORN in the North Country, the land of the Oak, and the Ash, the Bonny Ivy Tree, and—Handel's *Messiah*.

As winter approached the large Choral Societies with full orchestra filled the concert halls with overflowing sound, and small chapel choirs— albeit augmented—held forth in grim moorland bethels. *Messiah* dresses were handed down from mother to daughter, copies of the score were passed down three, four, five or more times, although the traditional *Messiah* singer worked his way through the oratorio holding his score prominently in front of him—closed.

However, I attended the parish church, and the parish church didn't involve itself in this annual musical orgy, or, at least, no one could remember the last time that it had.

"We allus leave it to th' Methodists," somebody said.

But we had a new curate, very keen, very new, and oh, so enthusiastic, one of those "Sporting Parson" types, the kind you feel has cricket boots on under his cassock and insists on being called by his Christian name.

He'd consulted the vicar; the vicar had said that it couldn't do any harm to call a meeting, and then had done the thing he always did, "got a headache" as his wife put it, and left Leslie (that was the curate's name) to face the meeting alone. For the first time, I think, Leslie was non-plussed.

He sat there looking rather sad, facing row upon row of representatives from the various church societies. Well to the fore, was the Mothers' Union, every corseted, quivering ton of it. The Church Council was there in force, the Scouts, the Guides, the church football team, Mrs. Howlett from the Sunday School, Meg who played leads for the Dramatic Society, and Albert Howarth, the oldest member of the existing choir (past his prime and a bit weak in his lower register now that the beer was taking its toll). Then there was Miss Jackson from the Girls' Friendly Society known as "Vinegar Dial" and three of us representing the Youth Club, an organization, need I say, much mistrusted by the Mothers' Union. We were apparently guilty of practically every crime in the book, from stealing their cups and saucers to white slavery. We turned up in force to show that we did really have the affairs of the church at heart.

Leslie opened the meeting, quite confidently I thought, considering that the odds were stacked so firmly against him.

"Now, do you think we could have a go at doing *Messiah*?"

There was dead silence, and everybody looked at Albert Howarth.

"We'd never get through it," said Albert deliberately.

Leslie looked puzzled.

"You see," said Albert confidentially, "we've got no strength in them contraltas. They're nowt but wind an' watter. Why, they fair near bust their stays if we do 'Cwm Rhondda'. If we went for th' *Messiah* you'd be carrying 'em out on stretchers."

"Well, I thought, actually," said Leslie, "that we might be able to *augment*."

"Whaat?"

"Augment, er, well, after all the Mothers' Union have a fairish little choir among themselves (the ladies of the Union rustled delightedly at this—a born diplomat was our Leslie) and after all, we've all heard the Youth Club sing, as they did at their Social some weeks ago. . . ."

That's a mistake, Leslie, I thought, you're not so clever after all. You know I did a take-off of a Mothers' Union coach trip, and you know six of them walked out in the middle.

"You're not thinking," said Albert, "of bringing in th' Methodists and such, are you?"

"Well, anyone who wants to could come along; after all, the more the merrier——"

Albert cut in smartly. "Then tha'd best think ageean, we don't fraternize at *this* church."

"Oh, come now," Leslie began, but seeing the looks on Albert's face, and the flush of indignation that was rising around the Mothers' Union he obviously decided to let that one ride.

"Well, I'm sure we can get quite a sizeable choir up within our own ranks, and perhaps some of you then will stay on afterwards to help out the church choir. After all it is very small, and you all have to work so hard."

"Happen so," said Albert after a pause that lasted just that bit too long to imply agreement with what Leslie had said.

"Perhaps your young friend Keith here could help."

"Happen so."

"Perhaps you could persuade some of the Youth Club to help?"

"Happen so," I said and Albert glared at me. I could have kicked myself for allowing that one to slip out, but I'd got carried away!

So that was how David, Peter and I came to join the choir, in order as the choirmaster put it to "bolster up the basses". That meant drowning the noise that Albert made. A couple of girls joined too, but they left after the first week. They said it wasn't much fun.

We rehearsed for six solid weeks, Mondays, Wednesdays and Fridays. We didn't practise Thursday because it was early-closing, and we couldn't on Tuesdays, because if we did we had to manage without our four Mothers' Union contraltos.

We were never far away from that *Messiah* music, and I remember one of our sopranos, who was a nurse telling me that she'd found herself humming "For unto us a child is born" as she walked down the Maternity ward.

We basses found, of course, that our main job was to hold up Albert when he'd been in the "Black Lion" before choir practice and to fill in for Tom Matheson next to me who, although he was a trained *Messiah* singer, used a very old copy of the work which had several pages missing.

The Sunday of the performance was foggy, very foggy. It came down from the hills early in the afternoon, curled round the grey stone church and very soon seeped in until it was almost impossible to see the West Door from the chancel steps. Now I don't know whether it was the fog that got into the old men's tubes, but when the time came, as the choirmaster put it to "brast off", there wasn't so much as a whiff of a bass, apart from us three youngsters.

"Well, you'll just have to sing up, lads," said the choirmaster. It was all right for him, he was a tenor. I suspected that it wasn't just an accident that Albert, Tom and the other four were missing. Albert hadn't liked the idea in the first place. Well, we obviously couldn't call the whole thing off. . . .

"Perhaps the others could sing quietly," I heard Leslie say.

The first few minutes were nerve-racking, to say the least. We'd had trouble right through rehearsals with those long bass runs of which Handel is so fond, and we found we had to sort of pleat them round the edges to make them fit. Still, when we got our second wind, we found, much to our surprise, that we were enjoying it, almost. It was most definitely

Handel versus David, Peter and myself, and I think that, for most of the way we just about had the edge on him.

The congregation rose, majestically, for the Hallelujah Chorus. Before this they'd been sitting there with that look on their faces that audiences the world over adopt on these occasions—a sort of "we've come to be entertained, so get on with it" kind of look. But this was *their* moment, and they held themselves taut, pink and shiny faces flushed in the hot lights.

David next to me whispered, "Well, it's every man for himself now, isn't it?"

He and Peter leaned towards me. "They think I know it" I thought to myself, and my heart sank.

We took a deep breath, smiled rather weakly at each other, and jumped in with both feet.

I can't honestly say that we were good. I can't even say that the choir as a whole was good—our sopranos sort of went off at a tangent at times, and the contraltos gave of their best, even though in some passages it *was* rather like a North Atlantic storm, and there was a nasty moment when the organist got his foot stuck, but afterwards everybody seemed quite pleased.

"Splendid, absolutely splendid!" said Leslie.

"Wonderful collection," added the vicar's wife.

"That'll give the Baptists something to think about," said Mrs. Worthington of the Mothers' Union.

"The basses triumphed against great odds," the choirmaster declared.

Now, I can't speak for the other two, we've never discussed it, never even mentioned it since that day, but I must confess that when the rest of the choir swept on to that last triumphal note of the Hallelujah Chorus, I still had a page and a half to sing!

Breakfast With Mohammed Abu Tayi

by Anne Sharpley

Ｉ T WAS LIKE this. I had a day to spare (Christmas Day as it happened) and I wanted to interview someone about T. E. Lawrence. I tried the usual blind alleys, then a guide who had just finished a two-year stint at Petra told me that Mohammed Abu Tayi, son of Auda Abu Tayi, was in Ma'an, 100 miles to the south. Now Auda Abu Tayi was the great Arabian brigand and warrior who was a key figure in the Arab revolt in the First World War and his son, Mohammed, a boy of eleven at the time, had accompanied his father and Lawrence throughout the campaign. "Well," I thought in my neat, nippy, news-minded way, "what could be easier than to dash down to Ma'an and have a few words with this son of the great Auda."

In a cold grey dawn—and there is something uniquely irritating about being cold in what one has fixed in one's mind as being a hot climate—my car raced along the new road to Ma'an. The drab desert horizon would have been perfectly straight had it not been for the earth's curvature, one could see so far. The railway, the Hejaz railway, which below Ma'an, Lawrence and others had been so effective in blowing up, ran with a chill needling directness across the emptiness. Ma'an was be-flagged, for by one of those happy coincidences that smack of compromise, Christmas Day is celebrated as the beginning of the Arab Revolt—so that Jordan's large Christian population need not be alone in their festivities. The Governor was holding a police parade, and the Imam was making a rousing speech. He introduced me to Sheik Mohammed Abu Tayi. One glance at him settled the meaning of the word "presence" for me for ever. Tall, broad,

216

black-bearded, hook-nosed, benevolent, stern, stately—what more does a man need to be.

He was wearing a red and white checked headcloth held down by the thick black cord of the *agal*. Under his black wool, gold-embroidered seamless robe, the *abaya*, he wore the Arab's answer to Western dress, which is the coat-half of a suit as we know it, with a long robe in suiting underneath. As a dashing and by no means phoney accessory he wore a pistol attached to a gleaming strap that crossed his chest.

In the Governor's office we sat down to talk of Lawrence—and as this was a festival the walls were lined with seated notables who nodded, commented, drank coffee and provided an audience for Sheik Mohammed's recollections. After two hours he said he must now go and make preparations to receive me. As I was by now eager to drive fifteen miles into the desert to Ghadir el Haj to see a point on the railway line where Lawrence had done one of his best day's damage, I didn't stop to consider what "receiving me" might be, but when I returned from that rare and rocky ride I learnt in fact that he had cut the throat of a young sheep, skinned it, had it cooked by his womenfolk, and it was all ready to be eaten. Only now did previous experiences of Arab hospitality in Egypt and Iraq come back to me in warning—but it was too late. I'd forgotten that to seek a favour of an Arab is to receive in return overwhelming un-repayable hospitality. You cannot casually "call" on someone in the desert. You become at once an honoured guest, a duty to be fulfilled, and what, by our standards, would be a damned nuisance. So, unwittingly, I had set a ceremonial meal of *mensaf*, as it is called, in motion. I was led to Sheik Mohammed's house, for like the modern sheik he is, he has houses as well as tents, cars as well as camels. "I would like to have welcomed you in the desert," he told me as we entered his big stone single-storey house with its wide corridor and huge salon, lined, as all Arab rooms are lined, with armchairs for those endless gatherings of coffee-drinking, world-settling males. Certain blights of our civilization spread fast and the plastic flower to my mind has got round the world quicker than neon lighting and tubular furniture even. Sheik Mohammed's salon boasted a huge bunch of plastic roses. His father's sword, elegant, fine and ferocious, hung on the wall, a craftsman's reproach to the roses. Sheik Mohammed's son led us to a sink at the end of the corridor where a bar of toilet soap was ready and the tap turned on. He stood by with a towel. As chief guest I was made to lead and therefore had a head-on start for the first of many mistakes I was to make throughout the meal. I omitted to wash my mouth after my hands and noted regretfully how my fellow-guests showily and expertly washed out theirs.

At the table we all stood in two groups around two towering piles of rice and mutton set on vast platters and surrounded by small satellite bowls of scalding hot sour cream. This was to be poured over the rice. Huge flat loaves of bread were handed out. My next gaffe was taking my bread in my left hand. I dropped it quickly. Nothing, I remembered, nothing must be done with the left hand while eating. Simultaneously I was already well into making another gaffe. I wasn't eating anything like voraciously enough. I *didn't*, largely because I was so stunned by the sheer beauty of the flavour of the food, and I *couldn't* simply because crushing the rice and meat into a ball neat enough to pop intact into your mouth is an expert job—and I was only getting expert towards the end of the meal. I was also waiting for a signal when it was time to stop. Now, I know it was my job as chief guest to bolt my food and rush away from the table leaving plenty for the Sheik and his household. Well there was certainly plenty left, but I had innocently allowed it to get colder than usual for them. I tore along the corridor once more to wash my hands, *and* my mouth this time, and we returned to the salon for huge apples and bananas and then some more of the perpetual delicious coffee in the tiny handleless cups that all share.

As we said good-bye, Sheik Mohammed, who had still to eat, said to me as though it were a matter of course that I would come again and put him to all this unthinkable trouble once more: "Next time you come," he said, "you must be so at home that you will feel like the host."

What a man! What a sentiment! What a Christmas Day breakfast!

Emmanuel

by Charles Melton

What is Christmas all about?
Some folk it seems know hardly 'owt
Save nuts and wine and turkeys fat,
But Christmas is not only that.
These have a rightful place no doubt,
'Twould be a doleful feast without,
But Christmas, blest with joy and mirth,
Means God is with us—here on earth.

USEFUL PUBLICATIONS

HOLIDAYS FOR THE ELDERLY. Send a s.a.e. to "Home This Afternoon", B.B.C., London W.1, for free brochure which includes holiday resorts with special facilities and organizations running holidays with a purpose; information about holidays for the disabled, blind, polios, diabetics, epileptics, multiple sclerosis, spastics, chest and heart patients, rheumatism and arthritis sufferers; medical insurance for under 75s, etc.

RETIREMENT. By Boswell Taylor and Robert G. Russell. Hodder & Stoughton, 3/6

FACING RETIREMENT. By a Country Doctor. George Allen & Unwin, 18/-

THE SPARE TIME BOOK. By Tony Gibson and Jack Singleton. Penguin, 3/6

RESIDENTIAL COURSES. Published twice yearly by the National Institute of Adult Education

LEISURE IN LATER YEARS. National Old People's Welfare Council (N.O.P.W.C.), 2/6

INCOME TAX AND THE ELDERLY. Issued free by the Board of Inland Revenue

A GUIDE TO VOLUNTARY SERVICE. By David Hobham. H.M.S.O., 3/6

AIDS FOR THE ELDERLY IN HOME AND GARDEN. National Old People's Welfare Council, 1/6

HANDBOOK OF INFORMATION. Scottish Old People's Welfare. Pergamon Press, 3/6

HEALTH HINTS FOR THE OVER SIXTIES. By Dr. Adrian Gillett. National Old People's Welfare Council, 6d. (includes exercises)

A FOOT IN THE DOOR. By Elizabeth Gundrey. Frederick Muller, 20s. (Exposes the ruses of doorstep and mail order salesmen)

VALUE FOR MONEY. By Elizabeth Gundry. Zenith Books, 5/– (101 ways to stretch your budget)

ULVERSCROFT LARGE PRINT BOOKS. To be ordered direct from the publishers F. A. Thorpe, Ltd., Artisan House, The Bridge, Anstey, Leicester. Price 18/– postage and packing

CLEAR TYPE BOOKS. A list is published by the Library Association at 10/–. They are made available to public libraries

FOOT CARE AT ALL AGES. By P. Read and H. Rosenstein. B.M.A., 1/–

HOUSING IN RETIREMENT. The National Federation of Housing Societies, 6d

HOLIDAY GUIDE FOR OLD PEOPLE. Issued by Scottish Old People's Welfare Committee, 1/–

ANNUITIES FOR THE RETIRED. Leaflet 1. Notes for the Retired Person 1965. The N.O.P.W.C., 3d

ANNUITIES FOR THE RETIRED. Leaflet II. Explanatory Notes. The N.O.P.W.C., 6d

BUILDING A BEAUTIFUL GARDEN. By Alan Taylor. Four Square, 3/6

NEW LIFE THROUGH BREATHING. By Knowles and Morgan. George Allen & Unwin, 16/– (includes exercises)

USEFUL ADDRESSES

BRITISH BROADCASTING CORPORATION, *Portland Place, London W.1.*

NATIONAL INSTITUTE OF ADULT EDUCATION, *35 Queen Anne Street, London W.1.*

NATIONAL COUNCIL OF SOCIAL SERVICE, *26 Bedford Square, London W.C.1.*

NATIONAL OLD PEOPLE'S WELFARE COUNCIL, (N.O.P.W.C.). *26 Bedford Square, London W.C.1.*

THE "OVER FORTY-FIVES" ASSOCIATION LTD., (job finding), *217a Kensington High Street, London W.8.*

SCOTTISH OLD PEOPLE'S WELFARE COMMITTEE, *10 Alva Street, Edinburgh 2.*

WOMEN'S VOLUNTARY SERVICE, *41 Tothill Street, London S.W.1.*

NATIONAL FEDERATION OF CONSUMER GROUPS, *13 Buckingham Street, London W.C.2.*

BRITISH ASSOCIATION FOR THE HARD OF HEARING, *Briarfield, Syke Ings, Iver, Bucks.*

BRITISH DIABETIC ASSOCIATION, *152 Harley Street, London W.1.*

BRITISH RED CROSS SOCIETY, *12 Grosvenor Crescent, London S.W.1.*

BRITISH RHEUMATISM AND ARTHRITIS ASSOCIATION, *11 Beaumont Street, London W.1.*

CENTRAL COUNCIL FOR THE DISABLED, *34 Eccleston Square, London S.W.1.*

CHEST AND HEART ASSOCIATION, *Tavistock House North, Tavistock Square, London W.C.1.*

MINISTRY OF PENSIONS AND NATIONAL INSURANCE, *10 John Adam Street, London W.C.2.*

MULTIPLE SCLEROSIS SOCIETY, *10 Stratford Road, London W.8.*

MUSCULAR DYSTROPHY GROUP, *26 Borough High Street, London S.E.1.*

NATIONAL ASSOCIATION FOR MENTAL HEALTH, *39 Queen Anne Street, London W.1.*

NATIONAL CITIZEN'S ADVICE BUREAUX COMMITTEE, *26 Bedford Square, London W.C.1.*

NATIONAL FEDERATION OF HOUSING SOCIETIES, *12 Suffolk Street, London S.W.1.*

PRE-RETIREMENT ASSOCIATION, *26 Bedford Square, London W.C.1.*

OPTICAL MISSIONARY SOCIETY (for the disposal of old spectacles), c/o *Mr. Albert Bailey, Hinstock, Marrow Brook Lane, West Farnborough, Hants.*

THE NATIONAL VARICOSE FOUNDATION, *10 Harley Street, London W.1.*

THE NATIONAL COUNCIL FOR THE SINGLE WOMAN AND HER DEPENDANTS, *71 Rectory Place, Woolwich, London, S.E.18.*

THE GOLDEN LINK (CLUB FOR DISABLED GARDENERS). *The Garden News, Stamford, Lincs.*